W9-BST-161

bad cat

by Jim Edgar

with
R. D. Rosen
Harry Prichett
Rob Battles

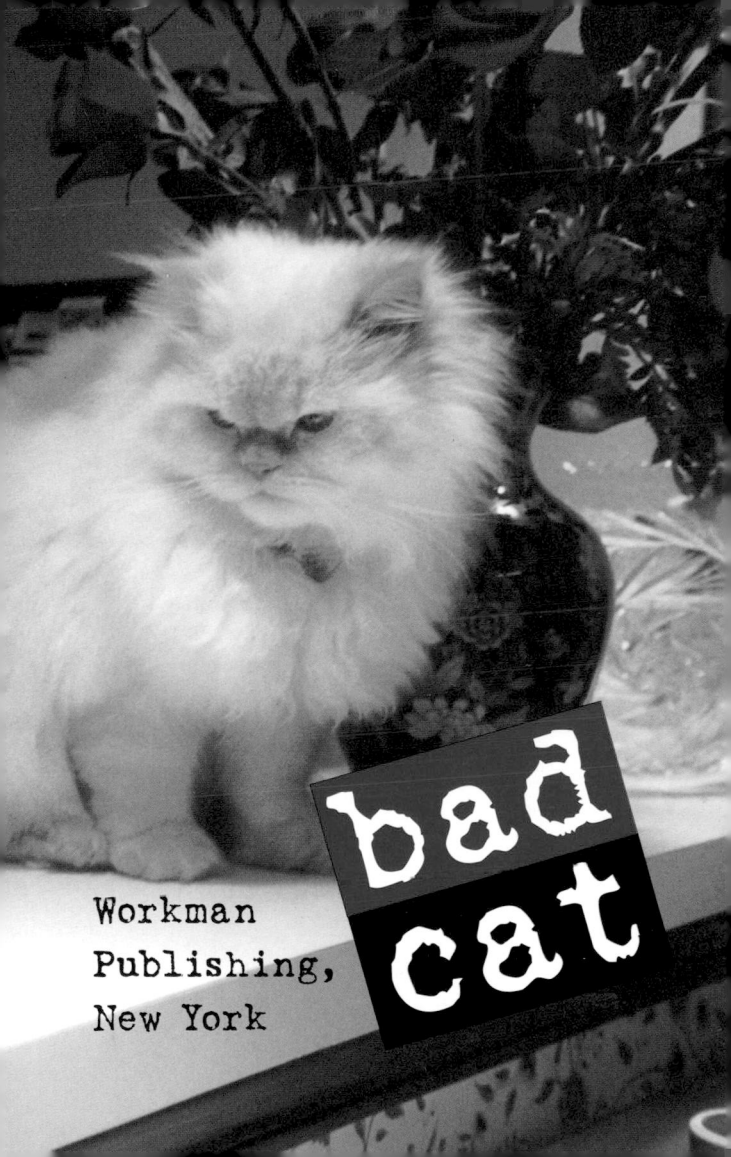

bad cat

Workman
Publishing,
New York

Library of Congress Cataloging-in-
Publication Data is available.

ISBN 978-0-7611-3619-4

Photo editor: John Blum

Workman books are available at special
discount when purchased in bulk for
premiums and sales promotions as well
as for fund-raising or educational use.
Special editions or book excerpts can
also be created to specification. For
details, contact the Special Sales
Director at the address below.

Workman Publishing Company, Inc.
225 Varick Street
New York, NY 10014-4381
workman.com

First printing October 2004

to Marlo Menez

Acknowledgments

Jim thanks Alex, Michelle,
his folks, and Beck Hansen,
another chump from L.A.
who made good.

Introduction

It is no secret that Cat owns *you*, and not the other way around. Why fool yourself with delusions of grandeur? Poor human, it's not your fault. Cat has been this way from the beginning, since the Garden of Eden. He gave the paw to Adam and Eve. He surreptitiously controlled the minds of thousands of Egyptians. He usurped Dog's position as household pet for the early Greeks. He has had his paw in the world's business for

millennia. But now Cat has had enough--enough of me, and he certainly has had enough of you.

Subconsciously, you know that inside that lovable ball of fur is a supercilious, sanctimonious, and always underestimated animal. He's not waiting to get out. He *is* out. Only perhaps you haven't noticed as you sit in your hovel littered with old pizza boxes, cigarette butts, and empty fo'ties of Schlitz malt liquor, watching reruns of *Star Trek,* petting the fluffy quadruped you have mistaken for your friend. Perhaps you need more evidence? Perhaps you are unclear about Cat's agenda?

I submit for your disapproval 244 cases in point--244 portraits of felines, their private lives laid bare by a snapshot and a few lines. See with your own eyes what Cat is *really* thinking, although he offers a gentle purr and a rub against your leg, or what seems to be a smile in your direction from across the room.

Want more? Then consult our Web site, http://www.mycathatesyou.com, where we reveal the secret thoughts and urges of thousands of felines in a terrifyingly candid fashion. As for the Web site, and the book you hold in your hands: Kids, stay away! And all *Homo sapiens* beware.

That is all.

Jim Edgar

Jim lives in Seattle, WA, and is deathly allergic to cats.

"I call it *fang* shui."

NAME: Bosco

AGE: 4

HOBBY: Breeding carp

"Never mind--it's a joke only frogs and cats would understand."

NAME: Peanut
AGE: 1
HOBBY: Internet dating

"The few, the proud, the hairless."

NAME: Jerry

AGE: 6

HOBBY: Racquetball

"Relax--I've done thousands of these procedures."

NAME: Dotty

AGE: 8

HOBBY: Watching *Silence of the Lambs* on DVD

"Take the freakin' picture already."

NAME: Scooter

AGE: 8 months

HOBBY: Crank calls

"Chicks dig me."

NAME: Mr. Fliegel
AGE: 7
HOBBY: Collecting Charlie
Parker on vinyl

"I still believe in the research we're doing here."

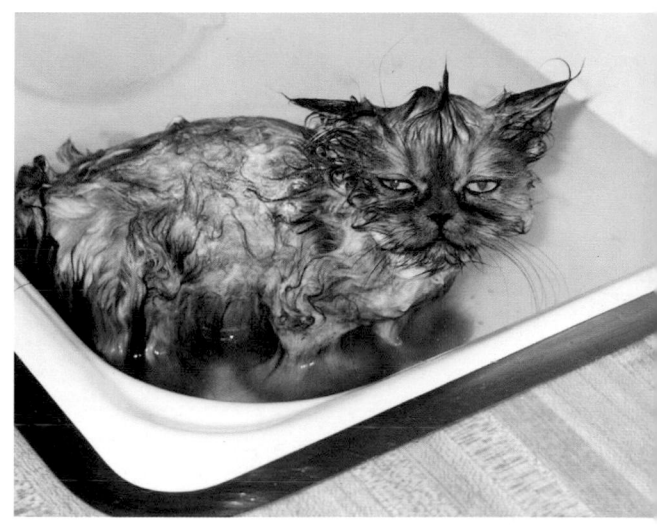

NAME: Alana
AGE: 12
HOBBY: Reading back issues of *The New England Journal of Medicine*

"Soon as the light turns green, let's see what this baby can do."

NAME: Chuck

AGE: 8

HOBBY: Collecting Beach Boys autographs

"She was naked when I came in."

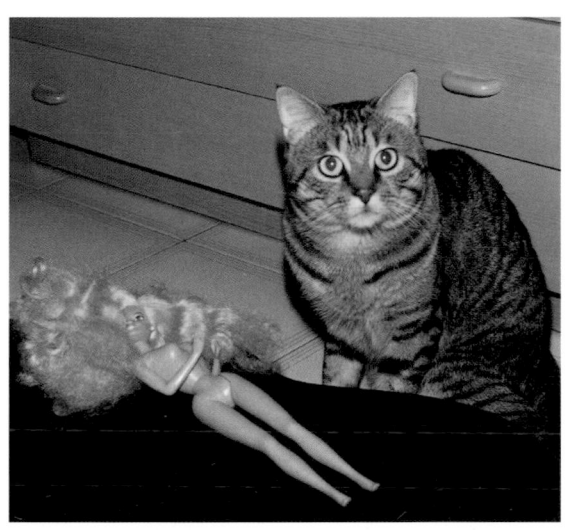

NAME: Clarence

AGE: 5

HOBBY: Frequenting flea markets

"I think the play date's over."

NAME: Rosie
AGE: 2
HOBBY: Shopping until dropping

"Where? Where does it say
'No peeing'?"

NAME: Buckles
AGE: 2 months
HOBBY: None yet

"I assure you lobotomies are making a comeback."

NAME: Brent

AGE: 14

HOBBY: Doubles tennis

"I said no tongue."

NAME: Yvonne

AGE: 6

HOBBY: Trying new bronzers

"I remember when I was the
only cat who could juggle."

NAME: Mr. Whiskers
AGE: 15
HOBBY: Collecting Emmett
Kelly memorabilia

"Oh, yeah, baby! Oh, yeah!
I like it like that!!"

NAME: Garth

AGE: 4

HOBBY: Scrabble

"Jerry Springer called. He wants us next Friday."

NAME: Shanika

AGE: 3

HOBBY: Creating personalized scents

"Take it from me, kid--by the third show you won't even know you're naked."

NAME: Terry

AGE: 3

HOBBY: Corresponding with prisoners

"What the hell is wrong with you? *Everybody* buys Girl Scout Cookies."

NAME: Suzy
AGE: 1
HOBBY: Helping little old Chihuahuas cross the street

"The only reason I do the pageant is for the free wine."

NAME: Melissa

AGE: 5

HOBBY: Collecting placemats

"If something should happen to me, my son Damian will take over the business."

NAMES: Damian (left) and Falafel
AGES: 1 month, 2 years
HOBBIES: Nursing; darts

"I like to watch."

NAME: Paula

AGE: 14

HOBBY: Popping chondroitin
and glucosamine
supplements

"I've left you this many surprises in your sock drawer."

NAME: Rusty
AGE: 3
HOBBY: Amateur magician

"This signal means, 'Start spraying.'"

NAME: Cummerbund
AGE: 1
HOBBY: Internet poker

"You never told me you had a sister."

NAME: Alistair

AGE: 4

HOBBY: Cruising kennel corridors

"Look what I downloaded--
and it's free!"

NAME: Maxie

AGE: 1

HOBBY: Instant messaging

"Oh my god!--where are my testicles?"

NAME: Tumbles
AGE: 6 months
HOBBY: Pooping behind the dryer

"I told you the clams were bad."

NAMES: Casimir (left) and Jujube
AGES: 9 months, 4 years
HOBBY: Seafood buffets

"I charge by the
half-hour."

NAME: Wanda
AGE: 3
HOBBY: Watching QVC

"I'm feeling it. Are you feeling it?"

NAME: Larry

AGE: 6

HOBBY: Leaping unexpectedly

"My ball. First down and whatever."

NAME: Wade

AGE: 4

HOBBY: Pencil sharpening

"One step closer and
Sidney's sausage."

NAME: Muncie

AGE: 4

HOBBY: Collecting old *LIFE*
magazines

"Mmmm. Salmon smoothie!"

NAME: Foodgie
AGE: 8 months
HOBBY: Watching *Iron Chef*

"I hate playing Operation
with your drunk friends."

NAME: Barbara
AGE: 2
HOBBY: Watching the lawn

"Next round's on me, Stan."

NAME: Penelope

AGE: 10

HOBBY: Eating other cats' food

"I come from another dimension, in search of mackerel."

NAME: Flek El Danizar
AGE: 1
HOBBY: Moving small objects with his mind

"Now you know why my name is Clog."

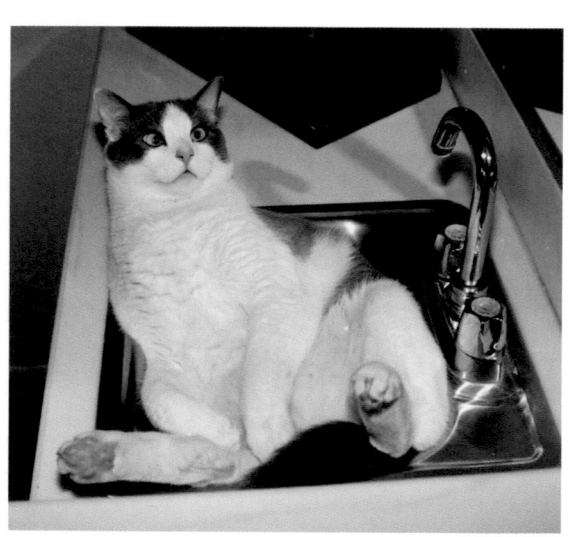

NAME: Clog
AGE: 7
HOBBY: Working with sheet metal

"If they fed me more I
could spell 'kitty.'"

NAME: Janet

AGE: 2

HOBBY: Buying too much lip
gloss

"Have you had your fun yet?"

NAME: **Gus**

AGE: **5**

HOBBY: **Chasing dust bunnies**

"Sonny says you talk too much."

NAME: Anthony

AGE: 17

HOBBY: Bocce ball

"Mrs. Claus told me to meet her here."

NAME: Alfie

AGE: 6

HOBBY: Just get me Mrs. Claus

"Blitzen's a putz."

NAME: Sarah

AGE: 11

HOBBY: Shedding

"Praise the Lord! I've been weaned!"

NAME: Niblet
AGE: 12 weeks
HOBBY: Speaking in tongues

"I'll have the burritos and a Corona Light."

NAME: Germaine
AGE: 3
HOBBY: Board games

"I think we're all making good progress, but we have to leave it there until next week."

NAME: Ruth

AGE: 14

HOBBY: Egyptology

"I told you--nobody wants
to hear Billy Joel."

NAME: Stacey

AGE: 10

HOBBY: Compulsive cleaning
around the litter box

"Make it look like this."

NAME: Stu

AGE: 8

HOBBY: Drinking the water in Mexico

"Man, thanks for leaving the Xanax bottle open."

NAME: Creamsicle

AGE: 7

HOBBY: Having staring contests with linoleum

"The first four times I killed it, I swear to God I had no idea it was rubber."

NAME: Appleby

AGE: 1

HOBBY: Browsing through women's magazines

"I found my drink."

NAME: Laverne

AGE: 8

HOBBY: Foosball

"I used to deal catnip
to the kittens at the
shelter."

NAME: Snax
AGE: 13
HOBBY: Trimming ear hair

"Here's to my recent neutering."

NAME: Algernon
AGE: 1
HOBBY: Bass fishing

"Ten the hard way!"

NAME: Hartley
AGE: 6 weeks
HOBBY: Betting on college sports

"Don't ask, but Klonopin was involved."

NAME: James

AGE: 2

HOBBY: Taking the metal detector to the beach

"I don't need to hear about your day. Just open the can."

NAME: Delilah

AGE: 3

HOBBY: Thinking about Abraham Lincoln's hat

"Hey, do I take pictures of you when you're on the pot?"

NAME: Mansfield
AGE: 2
HOBBY: Origami

"Hey, Lou! Mr. High Roller over here wants to know where he can find a coupla broads. Twins."

NAME: Bobby
AGE: 11
HOBBY: Rock climbing

"If you want to call us a cult, that's fine. The spaceship will be here soon."

NAME: Dick

AGE: 10

HOBBY: Neural-linguistic programming

"The gates of Hades swing wide and from the abyss comes Sassafras!"

NAME: Sassafras

AGE: 14

HOBBY: Asking if her ass is too big

"These killing sprees real_y
take it out of me."

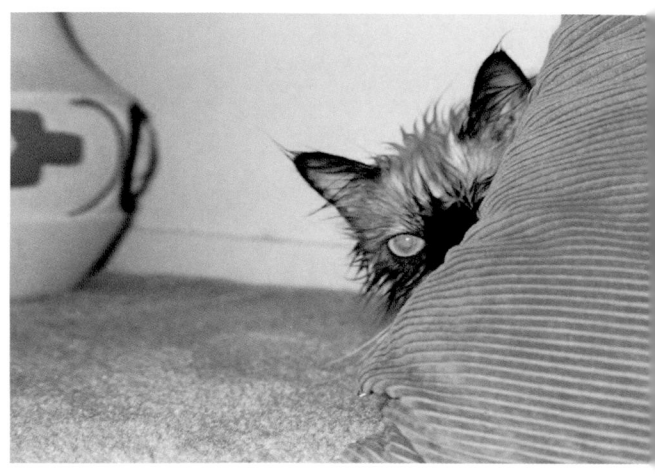

NAME: Roland
AGE: 5
HOBBY: Powdered milk fiend

"I would disembowel
you, but what to do with
the eight meters of
intestines?"

NAME: Lady
AGE: 1
HOBBY: Cheech & Chong
movies

"You think I'm cute?
Smell my tail."

NAME: Milo
AGE: 8 weeks
HOBBY: Looking tragic

"Santa told me to tell you
to go to hell."

NAME: Bootsy
AGE: 10
HOBBY: Hating

"Can you tell I've had
Botox?"

NAME: Stephanie
AGE: 12
HOBBY: Researching eating
disorders

"One bag of catnip, then I'll let you see the body."

NAME: Klaus

AGE: You're as young as you feel

HOBBY: Having "accidents" in the den

"Don't ever break the law in Turkey."

NAME: Eric
AGE: 10 months
HOBBY: Customizing scratching posts

"Got a light, sailor?"

NAME: **Fay**
AGE: **Old enough to know better**
HOBBY: **What do you have in mind?**

"I like a big dumb blonde."

NAME: Mike
AGE: 3
HOBBY: Candlepin bowling

"Harvey, crack me open
another cold one, will ya?"

NAME: Evelyn
AGE: 7
HOBBY: Watching Animal
Planet

"It's hard to say what fascinates me more, the drain or my own pathetic life."

NAME: Ronnie

AGE: 1

HOBBY: Who cares?

"When you're through, I'd
like to pee on that."

NAME: Gary
AGE: 9
HOBBY: Racing back and
forth in the upstairs hall

"I think the 'shrooms are
kickin' in."

NAME: Ravi
AGE: 11
HOBBY: Following The Dead

"There's no card--how do
you know it's for you?"

NAME: Clarissa
AGE: 8
HOBBY: Nipping

"I see kidney failure in your future."

NAME: Madame Farousha

AGE: 14

HOBBY: Trances

"I lost one to a Doberman and I chewed the other off myself."

NAME: **J.T.**

AGE: **5**

HOBBY: **Attacking strangers' calves**

"Mmmm. Blackened Mouse. A Cajun favorite."

NAME: Laura

AGE: 16

HOBBY: Bingeing on Cat Chow

"C'mon--stick your paw in
the socket. I dare ya!"

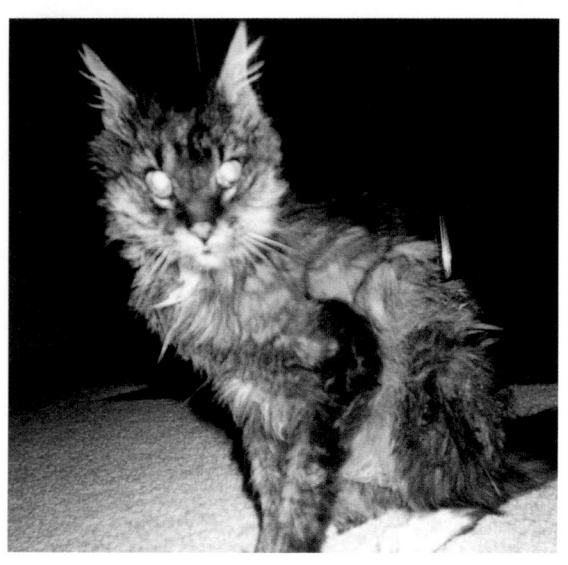

NAME: Wilson
AGE: 3
HOBBY: Reggae

"You're gonna love this place. Everyone's neutered."

NAMES: Jackie (top) and Flo
AGES: Both 4
HOBBY: Swing dancing

"From up here, I can see cleavage!"

NAME: Elmer
AGE: 2
HOBBY: Stickball

"Of course I believe it's never happened to you before."

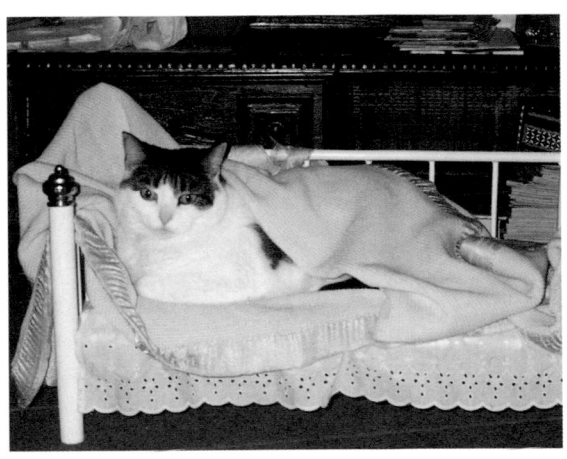

NAME: Judy
AGE: 2
HOBBY: Crystal healing

"There was nothing illegal
about that hit."

NAME: Lloyd

AGE: 3

HOBBY: Cheerleaders

"If eating kittens is evil,
then, yes, I'm evil."

NAME: Wilhelmina
AGE: 4
HOBBY: Needlepoint

"It's the hairpiece that
gets everyone excited."

NAME: Cliff

AGE: 13

HOBBY: Following the Arena
Football League

"After I drink a fo'tie,
I am poppin' a cap in yo
ass!"

NAME: Norm
AGE: 12
HOBBY: Catfishing

"I have opposable thumbs and I know how to use them."

NAME: Hitchcock

AGE: 8

HOBBY: Tracking down his biological father

"I said *shaken*, Miss
Galore, not stirred."

NAME: Otto

AGE: 10

HOBBY: Canoeing

"How many times do I have to say it? No luau."

NAME: Megan

AGE: 5

HOBBY: Collecting Fancy Feast labels

"This yoga pose lets me enter your room silently."

NAME: Ashaka

AGE: 7

HOBBY: Cross-stitching

"Remember to go light on the bleach. I have a date."

NAME: Heddy

AGE: 5

HOBBY: Looking at the Lava lamp in Sheila's room

"Oh, did I scratch your face? I'm terribly sorry."

NAME: Rikki

AGE: 2

HOBBY: Creating Thanksgiving dioramas

"This is Shelly's and my third booze cruise!"

NAMES: Shelly (left) and Dean Winkler
AGES: Both 1
HOBBY: Bridge

"Like I would know one day
from another."

NAME: Abigail
AGE: 4
HOBBY: Sand art

"Holy crap. Three reincarnations and you're *still* here?"

NAME: Eddie

AGE: 3

HOBBY: Knocking over expensive objets d'art

"Yeah, I'm a half-wit. Who's asking?"

NAME: Doodles
AGE: 3
HOBBY: Humming

"Isn't it ironic that this ancient Shaolin-style move is the last thing you'll see?"

NAME: Cookie

AGE: 1

HOBBY: Casting a spell on the neighbor's dog

"It's amazing what you can
see for twenty-five cents."

NAME: Mickey
AGE: 1
HOBBY: Mortal Kombat

"There was a problem in the teleportation chamber."

NAME: Anastasia

AGE: 9

HOBBY: Playing soccer with wads of paper

"Something stinks. Okay,
you two--which one?"

NAME: Zanzibar
AGE: 7 months
HOBBY: Lateral leaping

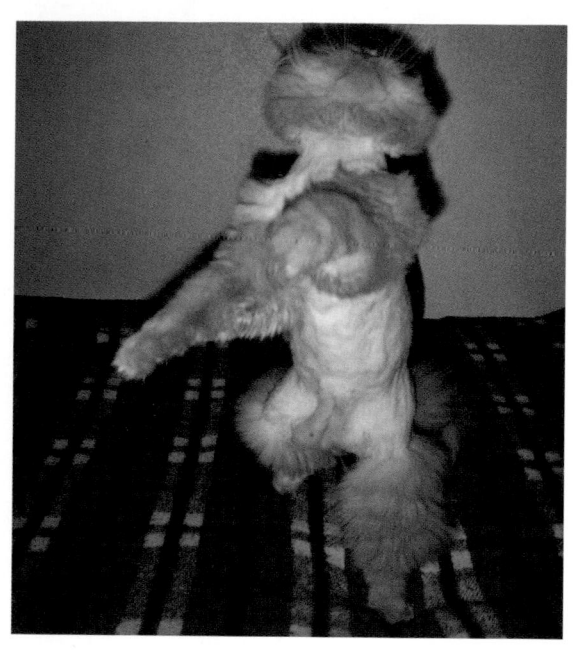

"Damned Ecstasy."

NAME: Macadamia
AGE: 6
HOBBY: Collecting glow
sticks

"I'm not coming out till Homeland Security tells me to."

NAME: Serafina
AGE: 4
HOBBY: Soy products

"The water's great, but the chlorine level's a tad high."

NAME: Sharlene
AGE: 11
HOBBY: Organizing kitchen drawers

"Please tell the victims'
families I'm sorry."

NAME: Smoky

AGE: 9

HOBBY: Making license plates

"Come over here. I want
to show you something
really cool."

NAME: Dorkhead

AGE: 2

HOBBY: Licking dinner
plates

"Philly, hand me the wirecutters."

NAME: Spengler
AGE: 8
HOBBY: Stripping furniture

"Damn--no radio."

NAME: Spanky

AGE: 5

HOBBY: Rewiring lamps

"When my kitty porn days are over, I'd like to teach ballroom dancing."

NAME: Mokey-Mokey

AGE: 2

HOBBY: The Texas two-step

"One word:
haaaaaaaaalitosis!"

NAME: Monica

AGE: 2

HOBBY: Working in pastels

"Bad cat? No, *Bat* Cat."

NAME: Blanche

AGE: 4

HOBBY: Letting people humiliate her

"I'm not listening.
Not listening.
Can't hear you."

NAME: Sashimi

AGE: 9

HOBBY: Pitying the fool who don't like Mr. T.

"Hey, guys--I found the erotica."

NAME: Bamba

AGE: 1

HOBBY: Getting in the lingerie drawer

"I've never even heard of Krispy Kreme. Look in the car again."

NAME: Lieutenant Feedalot

AGE: 7

HOBBY: Superhero comics

"My master went to the former Soviet Union and all I got was this lousy bust of Yeltsin."

NAME: Katnikov
AGE: 7
HOBBY: Reading Che Guevara

"That's right, Tweety--you did taw a puddy tat."

NAME: Stanford
AGE: 4
HOBBY: Slide piano

"Yes, officer, I know the
routine."

NAME: Ding Dong
AGE: 2
HOBBY: Squatting

"Say that thing about my
hair balls again."

NAME: Janice

AGE: 10

HOBBY: Being a love sponge

"I think I look foxy in a high waist."

NAME: Helene
AGE: 8
HOBBY: Sewing

"Pour some tequila into my navel and lie to me."

NAME: Lizzy

AGE: Young enough to get you in trouble

HOBBY: Sex

"That was fun. Now let's try 'whip.'"

NAME: Kevin

AGE: 2

HOBBY: Trying new cheeses

"Tell me you're sorry
again, but say it louder."

NAMES: Aquarius (left)
and Muddles
AGES: 5 months, 2 years
HOBBIES: The ball with the
little bell inside;
Greco-Roman wrestling

"Stop crying and cuff me."

NAME: Marilyn

AGE: 4

HOBBY: Decoupage

"At my age, it's nice just to cuddle."

NAME: Marmelstein

AGE: 14

HOBBY: Buying in bulk

"Last thing I remember is
the fourth margarita."

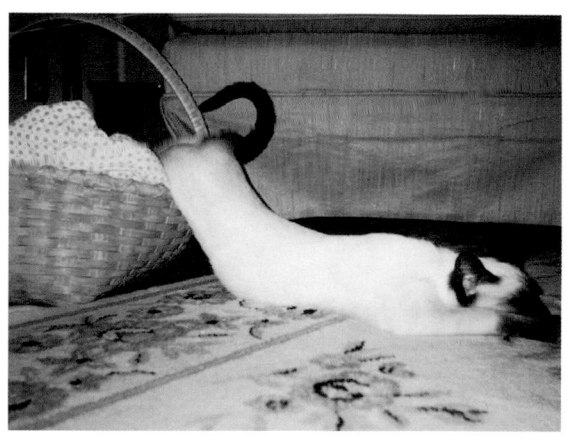

NAME: Lucinda
AGE: 1
HOBBY: Urinating

"I don't know, but it has to do with recombinant DNA and a fruit bat."

NAME: Crispy
AGE: 9 weeks
HOBBY: "Drunken-style" kung fu

"Boy, do I love ear!"

NAME: Francine
AGE: 1
HOBBY: Off-season clamming

"Three words: witness . . .
protection . . . program."

NAME: Victor Two-Chins
AGE: 6
HOBBY: Ceramics

"*I'm* a freak? You built it."

NAME: Misty
AGE: 4
HOBBY: Sleeping in front of
heating ducts

"Wow. I've never seen ones
like that before."

NAME: Brian
AGE: 3 months
HOBBY: Hiding in shoes

"Don't move, baby--I want
this lit just right."

NAME: Jerry G.
AGE: 1
HOBBY: Smoking meats

"I think it's time to go
back to rehab."

NAME: Petosky
AGE: 8 months
HOBBY: Eating freedom fries

"Too much gel."

NAME: Myrna
AGE: 1
HOBBY: Daytime soaps

"Actually, I think an all-cat production of *The Crucible* is long overdue."

NAME: Goody
AGE: 2
HOBBY: Playing the zither

"Speak for yourself. I'd still rather do *Guys and Dolls*."

NAME: Armando

AGE: 4

HOBBY: Pooping in the perennials

"I'm clown bait."

NAME: Rhoda
AGE: 4 months
HOBBY: Unicycling

"Ask me nicely or you're not getting your pants back."

NAME: Barley

AGE: 2

HOBBY: Wrestling inanimate objects

"I see what you're doing--
and I like it very much."

NAME: Agnes

AGE: 12

HOBBY: Getting pedicures

"Yes, Your Honor. I do understand the charges."

NAME: Buzzy

AGE: 3

HOBBY: Fondue

"Sure I could kill you, but that would be too easy."

NAME: Bartholomew
AGE: 17
HOBBY: Checkers

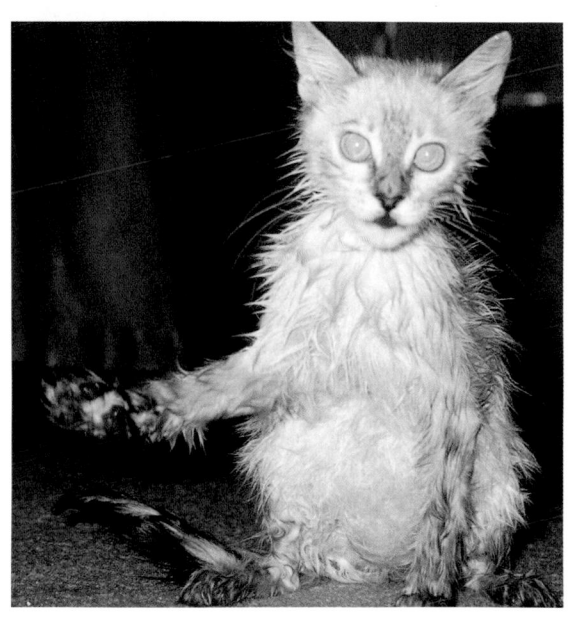

"The Three Mile Island
campground? Right over
there."

NAME: Sean
AGE: 9 months
HOBBY: Little League coaching

"I see London, I see France, I can see your underpants--wait--uh oh."

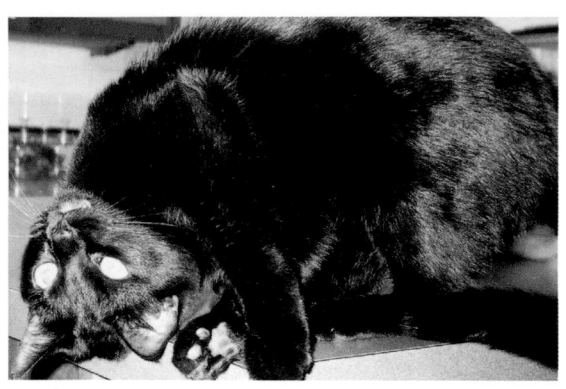

NAME: Klezmer
AGE: 3
HOBBY: Studying geysers

"What can I say?--he's good in bed."

NAME: Ariana

AGE: 4

HOBBY: Checking reflection in store windows

"In prison, I learned many crafts."

NAME: Happy

AGE: 9

HOBBY: Jailhouse tattooing

"Teddy and I do as we like, don't we, Teddy?"

NAME: Andrea
AGE: 1
HOBBY: Looking at motorcycle magazines

"Ken who?"

NAME: Roger
AGE: 3
HOBBY: Sardines

"Forget the donkey show.
Mojitos on the patio!"

NAME: Babs
AGE: 6
HOBBY: Making poi

"All I need now is a
bunker."

NAME: Dwayne
AGE: 5
HOBBY: Ammo

"Hold it right there. Put down the nail clippers nice and slow."

NAME: Gwen

AGE: 2

HOBBY: Using the Jedi mind trick

"This has been fun, but I'm scheduled to be spayed in half an hour."

NAMES: Sally (left) and Ethel
AGES: 4 months, 4 years
HOBBY: Mother-daughter mah-jongg

"You German Shepherds are
all alike."

NAME: Antonia

AGE: 4

HOBBY: Wearing lederhosen

"Now *that's* what I call catnip!"

NAME: Steve

AGE: 8 months

HOBBY: Zoning out

"I know that everything about it is wrong, but I just can't help myself."

NAME: Wyatt
AGE: 12
HOBBY: Pilates

"No matter how often I see it, it still disgusts and excites me."

NAME: General Burnside
AGE: 1
HOBBY: Falsetto hissing

"Touch my doubloons, matey, and I'll batten down your hatches."

NAME: Cap'n Hairball
AGE: 4
HOBBY: Removing barnacles

"That's it, Fred--that's my
last year working Macy's."

NAMES: Fred (left) and Homer
AGES: 8, 9
HOBBIES: Daytime television;
lighting matches

"It blocks out more than harmful rays. It blocks out you."

NAME: Philippe
AGE: Don't bother me
HOBBY: Not interested

"I know he's passed out,
but his mouth is open."

NAME: Gabby

AGE: 10

HOBBY: Dipping paws in the
fish tank

"This has been a blast. Now change me."

NAME: Doug

AGE: 2

HOBBY: Skeet shooting

"Note to self: stop after third lick."

NAME: Lisa

AGE: 9

HOBBY: Flinching

"We're not laughing with you. We're laughing *at you.*"

NAME: Cardigan

AGE: 7

HOBBY: Frightening small children

"I vomited on your wallet. Deal with it."

NAME: Perry

AGE: 1

HOBBY: Eating garbage

"My whole family's
big-boned."

NAME: Raffina
AGE: Middle years
HOBBY: Belly dancing

"Now you sleep with the fishes."

NAME: John "The Valve" O'Brien
AGE: 6
HOBBY: Lawn maintenance

"No more scurrying for you,
mister."

NAME: Felix

AGE: 6

HOBBY: Collecting mouse
heads

"I told you they were easy to install."

NAME: Lance
AGE: 4
HOBBY: Canning

"You will meet a hairless charmer and bear him six babies. Your career is about to take off. Avoid Scorpios."

NAME: Marcella
AGE: 9
HOBBY: Aromatherapy

"My therapist thought it would be good for my self-esteem."

NAME: Jasmine

AGE: 13

HOBBY: Nail-biting

"I'm sorry, Mrs. Carson, but these are made of plastic. I'll give you a dollar fifty for them."

NAME: Doc

AGE: 9 months

HOBBY: Making citizen's arrests

"Like you, this is where I do my best thinking."

NAME: **Julius**

AGE: 9

HOBBY: Imagining what it's like to be human

"Do *not* try that again. I eat first, then the ferret, *then* you."

NAME: Battista
AGE: 2
HOBBY: Running headlong into glass doors

"Now, class, a blow to this area will shatter the orbital bone."

NAME: Raul
AGE: 11
HOBBY: Soldering

"The one thing we miss about the carnival circuit is the drunken midget orgies."

NAMES: Sharon (left) and Karen

AGES: 6, 6

HOBBY: Trying not to breathe on each other

"Yo, yo, yo mutha! Respect
this shiznit!"

NAME: D.J. Hummer

AGE: 4

HOBBY: Waiting for the
Cubbies to win the pennant

"I have busts made of all my former owners."

NAME: Fiona
AGE: 19
HOBBY: Networking

"Trust me. The plan will work. Shit on the carpet until we get tuna."

NAMES: Madeleine (left) and Drew
AGES: Both 6 weeks
HOBBY: Carpet-soiling

"Smell it. I think I
stepped in dog doo."

NAMES: Louie (left) and
Stewie
AGES: 2, 3
HOBBY: Colonial cooking

"Gentlemen, I give you my masterpiece--a high-pressure meal delivery system."

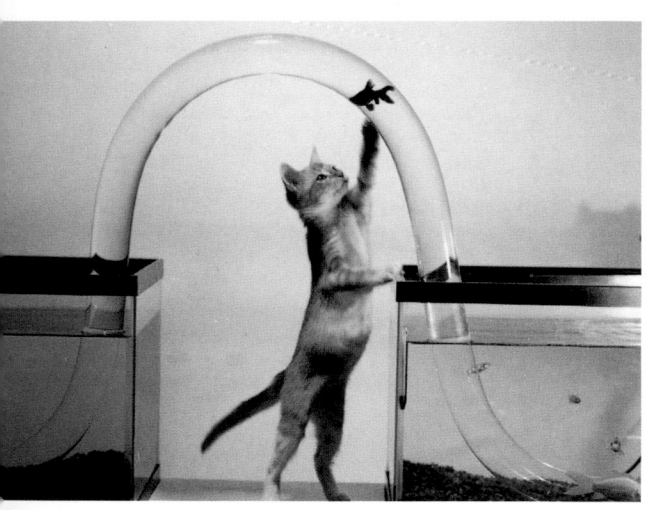

NAME: Myron

AGE: 10

HOBBY: Shortwave radio

"You're not flossing, are you, Boozer?"

NAME: Nadine

AGE: 3

HOBBY: Knocking back
jug wine

"I wish I hadn't killed the nice little doll family."

NAME: Chester

AGE: 8

HOBBY: Cop shows

"For my next impression,
I'd like to do a frittata."

NAME: Hector
AGE: 12
HOBBY: Autoharp

"The twins don't say much,
but they're very, very
thorough."

NAME: Svetlana

AGE: 3

HOBBY: Torturing ants

"He who denied it supplied it, but I'll still take a whiff."

NAME: Sebastian
AGE: 5
HOBBY: Flatulence connoisseur

"Just leave *The Watchtower* on the stoop."

NAME: Tangerine
AGE: 4
HOBBY: Vacuuming

"I'm afraid your
grandmother won't
be back."

NAME: Dominick
AGE: 4
HOBBY: Taxidermy

"This is my last show."

NAME: Mr. Moheb

AGE: 13

HOBBY: Cockfighting

"I'm through with all a ya--you and ya stinkin', shallow suburban lives."

NAME: Davis

AGE: 3

HOBBY: Elvis impersonator

"I hate candy. And now I hate you."

NAME: Marvin
AGE: 3
HOBBY: Light opera

"Polly want to get the hell out of my face?"

NAME: Jennifer

AGE: 6

HOBBY: Anger management

"Listen--the farmer takes a wife, the wife takes you, *you* take the cheese, and leave me out of it."

NAME: Clancy
AGE: 6
HOBBY: Washing left front paw

"C'mon, will ya--I'm on my break."

NAME: Sarge

AGE: Go away

HOBBY: Beat it

"What winning tickets?
These are mine."

NAME: Tito
AGE: 5
HOBBY: River tubing

"I feel sexy in my tiny sombrero."

NAME: Mitzi
AGE: 1
HOBBY: Making chili

"See? No canary."

NAME: Boz
AGE: 2
HOBBY: Baroque music

"How's it going down there?
You got enough air?"

NAME: Larkin
AGE: 3
HOBBY: Paintball

"Slowly now, and I want it all in crisp tens and twenties."

NAME: "Mr. Gray"
AGE: 5
HOBBY: Collecting dried turds

"Not for all the money in the world."

NAME: Debbie
AGE: 6
HOBBY: Kabbalah

"I sent them to your
ex-wife's lawyer. Why?"

NAME: June

AGE: 8

HOBBY: Balloon animals

"I hate myself for what I
now have to do to you."

NAME: Spencer
AGE: 8 weeks
HOBBY: Spearfishing

"I have already written your obituary. It's on the counter."

NAME: Margie

AGE: 1

HOBBY: Puppetry of the ancients

"I'll need a helicopter
out of here and five pounds
of kitty litter."

NAME: Unknown
AGE: Unknown
HOBBY: Not available

"Boo."

NAME: Feldman

AGE: 10

HOBBY: Testing monocles

"You should see me when I'm wet."

NAME: Seiji

AGE: 2

HOBBY: Biting the people who did this

"She doesn't care if I come home drunk, and that's all I care about."

NAME: Sugar Pie Honey

AGE: 17

HOBBY: Polishing wax fruit

"Oh, that's choice!"

NAME: Brenda

AGE: 4

HOBBY: Old Peggy Lee records

"All for one, one for all--
yeah, yeah, just get me
out of this hat."

NAME: Marbles

AGE: 4

HOBBY: Visiting living
history museums

"Don't shoot. Take the
wallet. It's in my left
pocket."

NAME: Cleveland

AGE: 3

HOBBY: Cursing in Spanish

"You guys get the reindeer.
The fat guy's mine."

NAMES: (left to right) Bucky,
Carrot Face, Moe, Irving
AGES: 6, 7, 1, 10
HOBBY: Holiday hijinks

"I smoke--that's why
they're yellow."

NAME: Herman
AGE: 7
HOBBY: Raising cherry
tomatoes

"Put your shirt back on."

NAME: Prince
AGE: 5
HOBBY: Bible study

"I can't wait to get out of
the Hamptons."

NAME: Mitch

AGE: 4

HOBBY: Looking at old issues
of *Maxim*

"It saw me and reared
up just like this. It was
definitely Sasquatch."

NAME: Andy

AGE: 8

HOBBY: Photoshop

"After this, I'll show
you something really
disgusting."

NAME: Melvin
AGE: 12
HOBBY: Scotch

"I love the smell of dirty underwear."

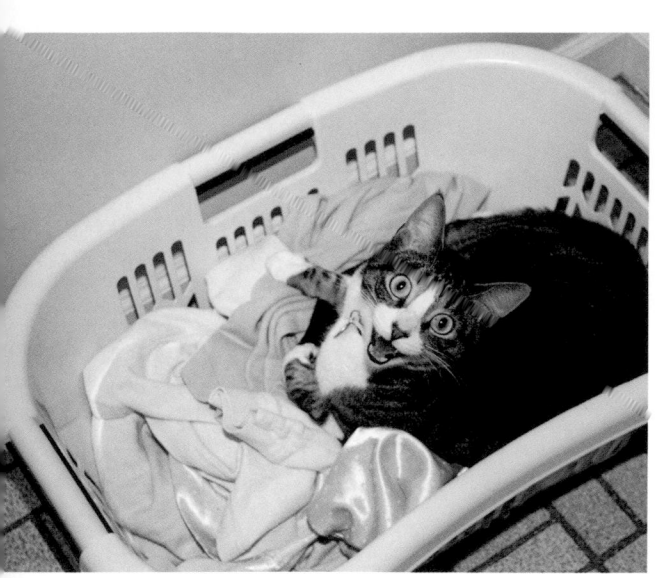

NAME: Erin
AGE: 2
HOBBY: Smelling dirty underwear

"That cheating tramp. Give me a double."

NAME: Arnold
AGE: 5
HOBBY: Monogamy

"Give me some of that good troll lovin'."

NAME: Amanda
AGE: 3
HOBBY: Listening to American musical comedy sound tracks

"I vant to suck your blood."

NAME: Petro

AGE: 12

HOBBY: Hitchhiking

"Good god! Please don't tell me the inside of my mouth looks like that."

NAMES: Marty (left) and Brad
AGES: 1, 4
HOBBY: Texas Hold 'Em poker

"Strangest damn funeral
I've ever been to."

NAME: Oscar
AGE: 6
HOBBY: Practicing scowl

"Hey, honey! Guess whose new neighbors are nudists?"

NAME: Jim

AGE: 14

HOBBY: Getting funky

"Sorry. Private party."

NAME: Meatloaf
AGE: 15
HOBBY: Nuffin'

"I'm picking up a signal
from Minsk."

NAME: Hermione

AGE: 3

HOBBY: Googling own name

"Could I look any *less* like a cat?"

NAME: Lex
AGE: 4
HOBBY: Old postcards

"I love older women, but
boy am I pooped!"

NAME: Nick
AGE: 4
HOBBY: Octogenarians

"For a can of sardines, I
go both ways."

NAME: Pat
AGE: 2
HOBBY: Welding.

"Bye Donner, bye Prancer-- next time bring more of that excellent North Pole weed."

NAME: Miranda

AGE: 2

HOBBY: Fantasizing about fish

"Mom! You're home early!"

NAME: Wicky

AGE: 3

HOBBY: Assault and battery
of upholstery with intent
to shred

"It *smells* like Betsy Ross slept here."

NAME: Shannon
AGE: 5
HOBBY: Social Security check fraud

"Take a whiff and guess
what I did."

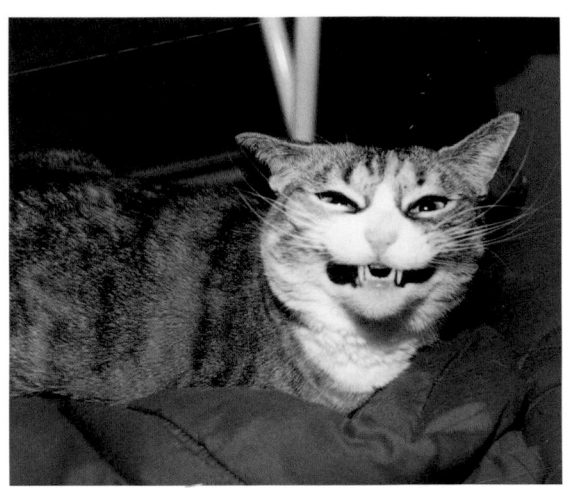

NAME: Blake

AGE: 9

HOBBY: Playing sock hockey

"Whenever I put the spider on my head, I feel irresistible."

NAME: Isabella
AGE: 3
HOBBY: Playing with own hair

"If you want me in chaps,
it'll cost you another five
bucks."

NAME: Dusty
AGE: 3
HOBBY: Japanese pop

"This *is* my smile."

NAME: Chaz
AGE: 7
HOBBY: Taking you for
granted

"You're fired."

NAME: Donald

AGE: 9

HOBBY: Preening

"And they said smoking crack was bad for me."

NAME: Precious
AGE: 3
HOBBY: Tearing open cereal boxes

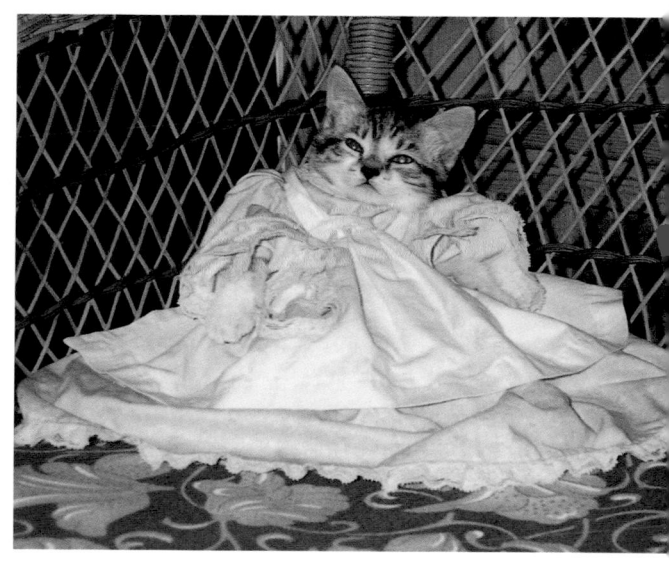

"What is it about our gang
colors you don't like?"

NAME: Franz

AGE: 5

HOBBY: Cooking with organ
meats

"Fritos, check. Twinkies, check. Bong hit, very check."

NAME: Wallace

AGE: 2

HOBBY: Tripping on the whole crazy universe

"Sure I believe in Santa
Claus. Especially the meat
on his legs."

NAME: Sludge

AGE: 2

HOBBY: Impressions of
famous cats

"Now it's seventy-*five* trombones in the big parade."

NAME: Gus

AGE: 8

HOBBY: Vegging out

"*Now* do you understand
why I prefer Hanukkah?"

NAME: Jenny

AGE: 1

HOBBY: Making dreidels out
of clay

"It's not too late to adopt,
you know."

NAME: Soba

AGE: 8

HOBBY: Writing haiku

"I'm not a bad ass. I *have* a bad ass."

NAME: Owsley

AGE: 4

HOBBY: Digging himself

"You'll stop laughing
when the rest of the
brotherhood gets here."

NAME: No. 616
AGE: 9
HOBBY: Marauding

"Thank you. We'll be here all week. Try the veal."

NAME: Tony Braciole & His Two Skeletons

AGE: 7

HOBBY: Craps

"Okay, who made the hash brownies?"

NAME: Eve

AGE: 4

HOBBY: Alternative medicine

"How was I supposed to know what's in a Long Island Iced Tea?"

NAME: Chi-Chi

AGE: 3 months

HOBBY: Experimenting with unknown substances

"Love to love you, baby."

NAME: Richie

AGE: 6

HOBBY: Cologne historian

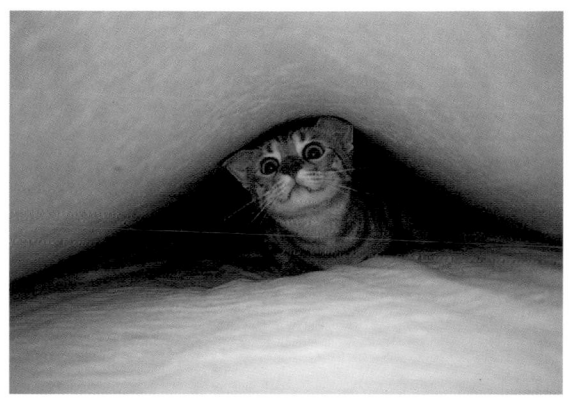

"So *that's* the 'horizontal mambo.'"

NAME: Herschel

AGE: 9 months

HOBBY: Identity theft

"I know this hasn't ended well for you, but I still think we've had fun."

NAME: Puff
AGE: 10
HOBBY: Iyengar yoga

The Death Penalty Targets People of Color

The American Bar Association three-year study concluded: "Every state studied appears to have significant racial disparities in imposing the death penalty, particularly associated with the race of the victim, but little has been done to rectify the problem." Other statistical evidence is consistent with this conclusion. Blacks make up 12% of the U.S. population, but they make up 48% of those on death row (55% of those on death row are people of color). The odds of receiving the death penalty increase by 38% when the accused is Black. Although 50% of murders involve white victims, 80% of death penalty cases involve white victims.

The Death Penalty May Constitute "Cruel and Unusual Punishment"

The Eighth Amendment to the U.S. Constitution states: "Excessive bail shall not be required, nor excessive fines imposed, nor cruel and unusual punishments inflicted." According to the U.S. Supreme Court, punishment is cruel and unusual if it is too severe for the crime, arbitrary, is rejected throughout society, and is not more effective than a less severe penalty. The U.S. is one of the few countries in the world that has executed minors under 18-years-old. In 2005, the U.S. Supreme Court ruled that the death penalty for minors offended "evolving standards of decency" and therefore constituted "cruel and unusual punishment."

According to the American Civil Liberties Union (ACLU), "The capital punishment system is discriminatory and arbitrary and inherently violates the Constitutional ban against cruel and unusual punishment. The ACLU opposes the death penalty in all circumstances, and looks forward to the day when the United States joins the majority of nations in abolishing it." There are five methods currently used to execute people—lethal injection, electrocution, gas chamber, firing squad, and hanging—and the ACLU argues that there are significant problems with each. Consider just a few examples of several botched cases.

A prisoner generally dies within seven minutes of receiving a lethal injection. Drugs for lethal injections in the United States were obtained from Europe, where the death penalty is illegal. However legal pressures and concerns from manufacturers in Europe have made traditional execution drugs unavailable. Thus, states have been trying experimental drug cocktails for lethal injections. In a 2014 Ohio case, Dennis McGuire received a lethal injection of two new drugs (midazolam + hydromorphone). The drugs took 26 minutes to kill McGuire, as he physically struggled, choked, and gasped for air. Also in 2014, a botched execution occurred in Oklahoma with an unknown mixture of "experimental" lethal drugs. The prisoner, Clayton D. Lockett, immediately began struggling after the injection was given, and ended up dying of a massive heart attack an hour later. His attorney said: "After weeks of Oklahoma refusing to disclose basic information about the drugs for tonight's lethal injection procedures, tonight, Clayton Lockett was tortured to death." In a 2006 Florida case, Angel Nieves Diaz died 34 minutes after receiving a lethal injection. The needle apparently went through his vein and into soft tissue deep in his arm. Eyewitness reports indicate that Diaz was still moving and attempting to speak (or, perhaps, scream) more than 20 minutes into the execution. In a 2006 Ohio case, it took over 90 minutes to kill Joseph Lewis Clark. Clark could be heard moaning and groaning from behind the curtain. In a 2007 Ohio case, it took over two hours and 10 attempts to kill Christopher Newtown. It took so long that Newton was given a bathroom break. In both the Clark and Newton cases, officials had difficulty finding a vein.

In 1999 Allen Lee Davis was electrocuted in Florida. "Before he was pronounced dead . . . the blood from his mouth had poured onto the collar of his white shirt, and the blood on his chest had spread to about the size of a dinner plate, even oozing through the buckle holes on the leather chest strap holding him to the chair." Florida Supreme Court Justice Leander Shaw said that Davis "was brutally tortured to death by the citizens of Florida."

Some people may be surprised to learn that the death penalty is far more expensive to implement than life in prison without the possibility of parole.

In 1983, the electrocution of John Evans in Alabama was described in a sworn testimony by his attorney: "At 8:30 p.m. the first jolt of 1900 volts of electricity passed through Mr. Evans' body. It lasted thirty seconds. Sparks and flames erupted . . . from the electrode tied to Mr. Evans' left leg. His body slammed against the straps holding him in the electric chair and his fist clenched permanently. The electrode apparently burst from the strap holding it in place. A large puff of grayish smoke and sparks poured out from under the hood that covered Mr. Evans' face. An overpowering stench of burnt flesh and clothing began pervading the witness room. Two doctors examined Mr. Evans and declared that he was not dead." "The electrode on the left leg was re-fastened. . . . Mr. Evans was administered a second . . . jolt of electricity. The stench of burning flesh was nauseating. More smoke emanated from his leg and head. Again, the doctors examined Mr. Evans. [They] reported that his heart was still beating, and that he was still alive. At that time, I asked the prison commissioner, who was communicating on an open telephone line to Governor George Wallace, to grant clemency on the grounds that Mr. Evans was being subjected to cruel and unusual punishment. The request . . . was denied." "At 8:40 p.m., a third charge of electricity . . . was passed through Mr. Evans' body. At 8:44, the doctors pronounced him dead. The execution of John Evans took fourteen minutes." Afterwards, officials were embarrassed by what one observer called the "Barbaric ritual." The prison spokesman remarked, "This was supposed to be a very clean manner of administering death."

In 1989, Alabama executed Horace Dunkins, who had been convicted of raping and killing Lynn M. McCurry, a 26-year-old mother of four. It took two jolts of electricity, nine minutes apart, to complete the execution. After the first jolt failed to kill the prisoner (who was mildly retarded), the captain of the prison guard opened the door to the witness room and stated "I believe we've got the jacks on wrong."

Life in prison without the possibility of parole keeps the public safe from killers, while eliminating the risk of an irreversible mistake.

The Death Penalty Costs More Than Life in Prison

Some people may be surprised to learn that the death penalty is far more expensive to implement than life in prison without the possibility of parole. Take the state of California, for example. The California death penalty system costs taxpayers more than $114 million a year beyond the cost of simply keeping the convicts locked up for life. In addition, California spends $250 million per execution. In addition to state costs, there are also federal costs. The federal court system spends approximately $12 million each year on defending death row inmates in federal court. Many death penalty cases involve a long, drawn out, complex, and expensive judicial process.

The Need to Abolish the Death Penalty

The family of a 14-year-old African American George Stinney Jr.—who was executed in 1944 for allegedly killing two white girls—has asked for a retrial in light of new evidence. Stinney's trail lasted only 3 hours, and the all-white jury issued a death sentence after only 10 minutes of deliberation. This case illustrates some of the major problems with the death penalty (e.g., it is irreversible, it targets poor people, it targets people of color).

Five countries in the world account for 80% of state killings: (1) China, (2) Iran, (3) Iraq, (4) Saudi Arabia, and (5) the United States. The other five countries in the top 10 are: (6) Pakistan, (7) Yemen, (8) North Korea, (9) Vietnam, and (10) Libya. The U.S. State Department recognizes 194 independent countries around the world, and the death penalty is banned in 140 of these (72%) as of May 2103, including Russia. As an aggression and violence researcher for over 25 years, I think it is time for the U.S. to join the other 140 countries that have banned capital punishment. Murder is a terrible crime that is never justified and should always be punished. However, I believe that the punishment should be life in prison without the possibility of parole, rather than the death penalty. Life in prison without the possibility of parole keeps the public safe from killers, while eliminating the risk of an irreversible mistake.

Why Conservatives Should Oppose the Death Penalty

Radley Balko

Radley Balko blogs about criminal justice, the drug war, and civil liberties for The Washington Post.

Though I don't always agree with him, I generally find Matt Lewis to be a thoughtful conservative commentator. His response to this week's botched Oklahoma execution, "The conservative case for capital punishment," is a good example. That is, it's a thoughtful piece of writing. And I don't agree with it.

The Death Penalty in the United States

But first, a few points where I think Lewis is correct. First, whatever your position on the death penalty—and I'm an abolitionist—these botched executions aren't a particularly compelling argument against capital punishment. As Liliana Segura has written here at The Watch, the background to the current debate over what drug cocktail states use for lethal injection is complicated and convoluted. We *could* quite easily execute people with methods that are quicker, painless and more humane. There are many reasons we don't. One is that the current drug cocktail has already been approved by the U.S. Supreme Court. Switching to something else would subject a state to years of court challenges and litigation (although that is what's happening now, and it will almost certainly intensify after this week).

Another reason is appearances. If your goal is to carry out a humane execution from the perspective of the condemned, the guillotine and the firing squad are far better than lethal injection. Because of the paralytic agent used in the lethal injection cocktail, we don't really know whether the people executed this way feel pain. And this obviously isn't something that can easily be tested. But the *humanity* component has never been about the humanity of the condemned. What we actually mean by *humanity* is that we want executions to be humane from *our* perspective. We don't want to feel icky about it all. A guillotine or firing squad conjures up uncomfortable images. Lethal injection, on the other hand, is a medical procedure. So long as the paralytic agent works, there's no twitching or convulsing and there's no blood. There's little evidence anyone has died. It's the method of execution that least resembles an execution.

The argument that the people who commit particularly horrendous crimes have simply given up their right to live is a compelling one, particularly when allowing them to live means they do so at taxpayer expense.

It's also worth mentioning that, as Segura pointed out, one reason states are turning to secret drugs obtained from secret and black-market sources is that anti-death penalty activists have been successful at persuading the manufacturers of the previously used drugs to refuse to sell them for use in executions.

Lewis is also correct when he points out that the declining percentage of Americans who support the death penalty (though it's still a majority) may in part be a luxury that's come with our dramatic 20-year drop in violent crime. We should reform the police and courts for high-minded principles like equality under the law, civil liberties and fair justice, but there's no question that it's much easier to rally support for reform when the country is less fearful of crime. (It also makes it much easier to bring politicians on board.)

Finally, while I don't agree with him, I do think Lewis' argument for retributive justice—that the most heinous of killers deserve nothing short of death—is the strongest argument in favor of the death penalty. There's very little evidence that capital punishment deters violent crime. The number of convicted murderers who escape prisons is also minuscule. But the argument that the people who commit particularly horrendous crimes have simply given up their right to live is a compelling one, particularly when allowing them to live means they do so at taxpayer expense. Death penalty proponent Robert Blecker often makes this argument. (Blecker is also consistent. He argues that the death penalty *should* be painful, and it should *look* painful.) It's a moral argument, and the only real response is another moral argument. Conflicting moral arguments can't be resolved with logic or data or other empirical evidence.

Government Control of the Death Penalty

But here is where I think Lewis' piece goes wrong:

> Other small-government conservatives and libertarians argue that it is inconsistent for people who already distrust big government to grant it the power of life and death over its citizens. As a conservative who believes in *ordered* liberty, and that it is a responsibility of government to protect its citizens, this argument doesn't dissuade me—especially now that DNA testing can and should be used to exonerate the wrongly accused.

This is the most glaring contradiction in conservative support for the death penalty, and Lewis really short-shrifts it. I agree with Lewis that protecting us from criminals is a legitimate function—and, indeed, is a primary responsibility of—government. But that crime-fighting is a legitimate state function doesn't mean that it isn't susceptible to the same problems Lewis points out when criticizing the things governments do that he believes *aren't* legitimate. When it comes to the trappings of public choice and political economy, the corruption of power and tunnel-visioned public officials, the criminal justice system is no different than, say, the Environmental Protection Agency, the Department of Education or the Occupational Safety and Health Administration. Actually, there *is* one important difference: The consequences of government error in the criminal justice system are far more profound.

Police, prosecutors and crime lab technicians are just as capable at conniving, malevolence and corruption as any other human being.

Lewis is correct about DNA testing: When it's dispositive of guilt, it can now be used to both exonerate the wrongly accused and to exclude suspects who otherwise would have been wrongly accused a generation ago. But DNA is only dispositive of guilt in a small percentage of criminal cases. It can be determinative in cases in which it's clear that the killer also raped his victim. It can also be important in cases where there was a clear physical struggle between the victim and the assailant. But DNA isn't a factor in most other homicide cases. And even when it's relevant, it rarely makes or breaks a case. Killers don't always leave behind DNA. A stray hair found at the crime scene that doesn't belong to the victim could have come from the real killer. Or it could just be a stray hair that wound up at the crime scene for innocuous reasons. And in cases in which the question isn't *who* committed the homicide, but *if* a homicide was committed (that is, whether a death was accidental or intentional), DNA will rarely be relevant.

DNA testing *has* shown us that within that small percentage of cases for which it does definitively establish guilt or innocence, there's an alarmingly high rate of error. DNA testing has shown, for example, that methods of forensic analysis and types of evidence that we once thought foolproof or relatively certain are far from either. DNA testing has exonerated people who were convicted because of bite-mark matching, hair and fiber matching, blood-type matching, testimony from jail-house informants, eyewitness testimony and even fingerprint matching. (This list isn't comprehensive, of course.) Here's the thing: If the state's misuse of this sort of evidence is capable of convicting innocent people in the small percentage of criminal cases for which DNA testing is dispositive of guilt, it's almost certainly causing wrongful convictions in all of those other cases for which DNA testing is less important or irrelevant. In other words, DNA testing isn't a panacea. It's a wake-up call.

Find the exonorees who served decades in prison before they were cleared and released. Now ask them if they'd rather have been executed.

The Problem of Error

Lewis makes clear that he only supports the death penalty for the most heinous of crimes, and only for those crimes for which the defendant's guilt is certain. At first blush, it's hard to quarrel with that position. The rub is that we'll always need to draw that line somewhere. *How* heinous must the crime be? And *how* certain of guilt must we be? There have been more than a few exonerations in cases in which it seemed unimaginable that the accused people could possibly have been innocent. And yet they were. We now know that prosecutors and police are capable of fabricating and planting evidence. Not that it's necessarily common, but it happens. That means that even DNA cases aren't necessarily iron-clad. The science behind the testing may be certain, but the gathering and testing of evidence will always be done by humans and be subject to all the biases, imperfections and temptations to corruption that come with them. Or to put it in terms with which conservatives might better relate: Police, prosecutors and crime lab technicians are just as capable at conniving, malevolence and corruption as any other human being. There's nothing transformative about a government paycheck that ensures altruism, honesty or goodness; the same goes with giving someone a badge or asking him or her to swear an oath.

This was the point of my poll question here earlier this week. If you support the death penalty, you have to recognize that it will be administered by human beings, who are flawed, and then you have to acknowledge the possibility that no system of justice can be perfect. This means that over time, the probability of executing an innocent person eventually reaches 1. The question, then, isn't whether you believe an innocent person has ever been executed. The question is how many innocent people you're comfortable executing.

Finally, Lewis doesn't explicitly make this argument, but I've seen versions of it made by others on the right: *There will always be errors. So there will always be injustice. We don't scrap the whole idea of punishment because some innocents may be wrongly convicted. So why do away with a specific form of punishment?*

The answer is that death is irreversible. It's an obvious answer, but it's an important one. With a life sentence, there's always the chance to catch the mistake and ameliorate it. (It can never be fully corrected, of course.) Death penalty supporters make the argument that for an innocent person, life in prison is a punishment that's worse than death. There's a pretty easy way to test that theory. Find the exonorees who served decades in prison before they were cleared and released. Now ask them if they'd rather have been executed. I've asked a few this question. The response was some version of *Are you nuts?* I'd be surprised if you could find a single exoneree who would answer *yes*. I'd be astonished if you could find more than a couple.

Criminal Justice System Reform

One more point. I have no doubt that Lewis is sincere when he says his support for capital punishment is contingent on cleaning up the criminal justice system, fixing the mistakes we've discovered and ensuring that only the most vicious killers are executed, and in only the cases where guilt is an absolute certainty. If Lewis is up for prodding his ideological fellow travelers to support policies such as requiring a heightened burden of proof in capital cases, or restricting death penalty cases to a very narrow class of exceptionally horrific crimes (as a task force in Ohio recently recommended after a series of exonerations), that at least would be a good start.

The problem is that the politicians he and other conservatives support—the (mostly) Republican officials and legislators in states like Tennessee, Missouri, California, Florida and Arizona, among others—are *expanding* the number of crimes for which prosecutors can seek the death penalty and looking to *speed* up the rate at which they execute people. (In Ohio, prosecutors and conservative politicians have rejected the task force's recommendations.) They're doing this even as we're still discovering wrongful convictions in those states and before they've bothered to pass meaningful reforms to address the problems that led to those convictions. In fact, in many cases, they're *rejecting* reform at the same time that they're trying to churn out more executions. Even low-cost, common-sense reforms such as recording police interrogations or ensuring double-blind eyewitness lineups are tough to get by Republican politicians. (Democrats aren't much better, but that's a separate discussion.) In other words, Lewis's position is defensible in the abstract. But that isn't the way things are playing out on the ground.

People who subscribe to different belief systems sometimes have irreconcilable views on public policy issues with a strong moral component. The death penalty is one of those issues. But conservatives are supposed to be skeptical of government. That *is* a fundamental part of their belief system. And, except perhaps war, there's no issue for which the consequences of government error or abuse of power are more absolute, irreversible and profound. Even if they support the idea of capital punishment in principle, it ought to be one of the *last* issues for which conservatives would be willing to abandon that skepticism. Yet it seems to be one of the issues for which their skepticism is most negotiable.

The Death Penalty Is Too Costly for Society

Richard C. Dieter

Richard C. Dieter is executive director of the Death Penalty Information Center.

One of the most common misperceptions about the death penalty is the notion that the death penalty saves money because executed defendants no longer have to be cared for at the state's expense. If the costs of the death penalty were to be measured at the time of an execution, that might indeed be true. But as every prosecutor, defense attorney, and judge knows, the costs of a capital case begin long before the sentence is carried out. Experienced prosecutors and defense attorneys must be assigned and begin a long period of investigation and pre-trial hearings. Jury selection, the trial itself, and initial appeals will consume years of time and enormous amounts of money before an execution is on the horizon.

The Costs of the Death Penalty

The death penalty is an exceedingly expensive part of the criminal justice system because it is necessarily very inefficient. I say "necessarily" because, as the U.S. Supreme Court has repeatedly said when it comes to punishment, "death is different." This means that the ordinary system of due process is insufficient in capital cases. Virtually every step in the criminal justice process will take longer in a death penalty case and be more complicated. In terms of costs, it means that whatever expenses there are in an ordinary criminal case, they will be much higher in a capital case. More experienced lawyers will be needed, more experts will be employed, more questions will be asked of potential jurors, more time will be taken for the trial and appeals. The end result is that very few of the people selected for death penalty prosecution will ever be executed. And yet, the costs of every one of those potential cases must be counted to arrive at the true cost of the death penalty.

The cost of our country's going to the moon cannot be restricted to the expense of a single rocket and lander. We have to include all the experimental flights, all the research, all the failures and partial successes that necessarily precede such a complicated venture. The same is true for the death penalty. A typical state has hundreds of cases that are eligible for the death penalty. A formal capital prosecution will be undertaken in less than half of these cases; much fewer will go to trial; only some will be sentenced to death; and very, very few will survive appeals and result in an execution. Nebraska is a good example. According to an article in the *Omaha World-Herald*, during a period of almost 35 years after the death penalty was reinstated in 1973, 205 murder cases were eligible for the death penalty; 31 of those resulted in death sentences; and just 3 resulted in executions, though none since 1997. The extra costs of the death penalty were present in all of the cases where the prospect of the death penalty was raised, even in cases in which the death penalty was sought but a life sentence was given. Across the country, only about 15% of those who have been sentenced to death have been executed.

[The] costs reflect the reality that most capital prosecutions never result in a death sentence, and most death sentences do not result in an execution.

There is no national figure for the cost of the death penalty. Every state study is dependent on that state's laws, pay scales, and the extent to which it uses the death penalty. Studies have been conducted by research organizations, public defender offices, legislative committees, and the media. Researchers have employed different approaches, using different assumptions. However, *all of the studies conclude that the death penalty system is far more expensive than an alternative system in which the maximum sentence is life in prison.*

Some recent cost studies provide an example of how much the death penalty can cost over the years that the policy is in existence:

- In Maryland, a comprehensive cost study by the Urban Institute in 2008 estimated the extra costs to taxpayers for death penalty cases prosecuted between 1978 and 1999 to be $186 million. Based on the 5 executions carried out in the state, this translates to a cost of $37 million per execution. The complete cost of a death sentence (trial, appeals, incarceration on death row) was estimated to be $3 million. The cost for a comparable case in which death was not sought was $1.1 million (including life-time incarceration). (The state is on the verge of abolishing the death penalty.)

- In New York and New Jersey, the high costs of capital punishment were one factor in those states' decisions to abandon the death penalty. New York spent about $170 million over 9 years and had no executions. New Jersey spent $253 million over a 25-year period and also had no executions. In such states the cost per execution obviously cannot be calculated, but even assuming they eventually reached one execution every other year, and continued the annual expenditures indicated in their studies, the cost per execution would be in the $20-to-$40 million range.

- In 2008, the California Commission on the Fair Administration of Justice released an exhaustive report on the state's capital punishment system. The report found that the state was spending $137 million per year on the death penalty. The Commission estimated a comparable system that sentenced the same inmates to a maximum punishment of life without parole would cost only $11.5 million per year. Since the number of executions in California has averaged less than one every two years since the death penalty was reinstated in 1977, the cost *for each execution* is over $250 million. The state has also indicated it needs another $400 million to construct a new death row.

The death penalty cost California $90 million annually beyond the ordinary expenses of the justice system, of which $78 million was incurred at the trial level.

It is important to emphasize the high costs per execution do not mean that executions themselves are expensive, or that pursuing one execution will cost tens of millions of dollars. Rather, these costs reflect the reality that most capital prosecutions never result in a death sentence, and most death sentences do not result in an execution.

Death Penalty Costs Are Increasing

The costs of the death penalty when measured per execution are rising. In 1988, the *Miami Herald* estimated that the costs of the death penalty in Florida were $3.2 million per execution, based on the costs and rate of executions at that time. But today there are more people on death row, fewer executions per year, and higher overall costs, all contributing to a significantly *higher cost per execution*. A recent estimate by the *Palm Beach Post* found a much higher cost per execution: Florida now spends $51 million a year over what it would spend to punish all first-degree murderers with life in prison without parole. Based on the 44 executions Florida carried out from 1976 to 2000, that amounts to a cost of $24 million for each execution, a significant rise from earlier projections.

A similar increase appears in California. In 1988, the *Sacramento Bee* found that the death penalty cost California $90 million annually beyond the ordinary expenses of the justice system, of which $78 million was incurred at the trial level. But the costs have increased sharply since then. As noted above, the costs now are estimated at $137 million per year.

It is also revealing to examine the costs of specific features of the death penalty system, as revealed through state and federal studies:

- In Maryland, the 106 cases in which a death sentence was sought but *not imposed* will cost the state $71 million. This extra cost is solely due to the fact that the death penalty was pursued, even though the ultimate outcome was a life or long-term prison sentence.

- The average cost for just the *defense* at trial in a federal death case is $620,932, about 8 times that of a noncapital federal murder case.

- In Kansas, the *trial costs* for death cases were about 16 times greater than for non-death cases ($508,000 for death case; $32,000 for non-death case). The appeal costs for death cases were 21 times greater.

- In California, the *cost of confining one inmate to death, row* is $90,000 per year more than the costs of incarcerating the same inmate in a maximum-security prison. Death row inmates require higher security, often in single cells, where meals and other essentials are brought to them daily. This is a very inefficient means of confinement. With California's current death row population of over 700, that amounts to at least $63 million annually.

The Opportunity Costs of Death Penalty Cases

Generally, offices involved in the prosecution or defense of criminal cases expand or contract according to the work that must be done. The extra time required by death penalty cases typically has caused the size and budgets of such offices to increase, but not every cost associated with the death penalty appears as a line item in the state budget. Prosecutors, who are not paid by the hour, have been reluctant to divulge the time and related expenses reflecting their part in capital cases. Judges and public defenders are usually salaried employees who will be paid the same amount whether assigned to death penalty cases or other work. But a study would be incomplete if it did not include the *extra time* that pursuing the death penalty takes compared to cases prosecuted without the death penalty in calculating costs.

Whatever savings are produced through [plea bargaining] are overwhelmed by the costs of preparing for a death penalty prosecution, even if it never goes to trial.

If it takes 1,000 hours of state-salaried work to arrive at a death sentence and only 100 hours to have the same person sentenced to life without parole, the 900 hours difference is a state asset. If the death penalty is eliminated, the county or the state can decide whether to direct those employee-hours to other work that had been left undone, perhaps to pursue cold cases, or choose to keep fewer employees. There is a financial dimension to all aspects of death penalty cases, and proper cost studies take these "opportunity costs" into account.

The Effect of Plea Bargaining

One asserted refutation that has been offered to the high cost of the death penalty is that the threat of this punishment produces financial savings because defendants are more likely to accept plea bargains, thus avoiding the cost of a trial. However, whatever savings are produced through this ethically questionable practice are overwhelmed by the costs of preparing for a death penalty prosecution, even if it never goes to trial.

Some of the most thorough cost analyses conducted over the past 15 years specifically address plea bargaining as an area that could affect the costs of the death penalty, including those in North Carolina, Indiana, Kansas, and California, though some considered it too speculative to measure. These studies nevertheless concluded that the death penalty added significantly to the costs of the criminal justice system.

The dubiousness of any savings from this practice is underscored by a federal death penalty cost study. The Judicial Conference of United States concluded that the average cost of representation in federal death penalty cases *that resulted in plea bargains* was $192,333. The average cost of representation in cases that were eligible for the death penalty but in which the *death penalty was not sought* was only $55,772. This indicates that *seeking* the death penalty raises costs, even when the case results in a plea bargain. It would be far cheaper to pursue murder cases if the death penalty were never on the table, even taking some non-capital cases to trial, than to threaten the use of the death penalty to induce a plea bargain because the legal costs of preparing for a death penalty case far exceed the costs of a non-death penalty trial.

It is not just the price tag of the death penalty that has drawn concern, but rather what is society getting back from capital punishment for all the millions of dollars invested?

Moreover, data from some states refute the notion that the death penalty increases the incentive to plea bargain. Prosecutors in New Jersey said that abolition of the death penalty there in 2007 has made no difference in their ability to secure guilty pleas. In Alaska, where plea bargaining was abolished in 1975, a study by the National Institute of Justice found that since the end of plea bargaining, "guilty pleas continued to flow in at nearly undiminished rates. Most defendants pled guilty even when the state offered them nothing in exchange for their cooperation."

In addition, the practice of charging the death penalty for the purpose of obtaining plea bargains is an unethical and unconstitutional interference with a defendant's Sixth Amendment right to trial. It risks convicting innocent defendants who plead guilty solely to avoid the possibility of a death sentence—which has occurred on numerous occasions, including in Nebraska.

Some have argued that a consideration of costs has no place in our pursuit of justice. However, it is not just the price tag of the death penalty that has drawn concern, but rather what is society getting back from capital punishment for all the millions of dollars invested? And where else could that money be spent that might produce a greater benefit? The primary purpose of the criminal justice system is to make society safer. All aspects of this system—preventing crime, apprehending offenders, trials, and punishment—have costs. Cutbacks in any part of the criminal justice system can potentially result in a less safe society. Choices have to be made. The death penalty is the most expensive part of the system on a per-offender basis. Millions are spent seeking to achieve a single death sentence that, even if imposed is unlikely to be carried out. Money the police desperately need for more effective law enforcement is wasted on the death penalty....

The Time Taken for Death Penalty Cases

Much of the delay in carrying out the death penalty is a healthy caution resulting from the near executions of innocent people. It is also the result of years of a very broad use of capital punishment, which created large death rows and a backlog of cases in the appellate courts.

For executions carried out in 2010, the average time between sentencing and execution was 15 years, the longest time for any year since the death penalty was reinstated in 1976. Even in Texas, the time between sentencing and execution is ten years. In some states, inmates are on death row for 20 or even 30 years awaiting execution. About 275 inmates have been on death row for 24 years or more.

In most states, executions are rare, the delay between sentencing and executions has lengthened, and the cost of death penalty cases has grown considerably.

This extensive delay results in the imposition of two sentences on the defendant: a life sentence in highly restricted confinement, *and* a death sentence. Of the capital cases that have been concluded, only about one-quarter of those sentenced to death were executed. Three-quarters of the defendants were permanently removed from death row for other reasons.

Such a system is enormously expensive for the state and a source of frustration for many. Death penalty cases are very costly to prosecute and defend compared to similar cases without the death penalty. When a death sentence is handed down, there will be years of expensive appeals and a form of incarceration that is much more expensive than the costs in general population. And at the end of the process, most defendants will end up with a life sentence anyhow—though one achieved through the most expensive process in the criminal justice system—the death penalty. Those left with a death sentence will probably not be the worst offenders, but rather an unfortunate few determined by arbitrary factors. Even for many supporters of capital punishment, this system makes little sense.

It has also created skepticism among the public regarding the value of such a nebulous form of justice. Indeed, some family members have remarked that, given the extensive time, the unpredictability of the outcome, and the painful re-living of the tragedy that inevitably accompanies this process, it would have been better if a life sentence had been imposed in the first place. . . .

The death penalty in the United States has become un-wieldy. In most states, executions are rare, the delay between sentencing and executions has lengthened, and the cost of death penalty cases has grown considerably. Yet for all this additional effort, death penalty cases are still prone to error and the risk of executing an innocent person remains. The public and the families of victims have a right to be frustrated with this system. But there is no simple way to reduce delays and costs while ensuring that innocent lives are protected and that the system works fairly. This dilemma is one of the principal reasons that the use of the death penalty has declined so dramatically in recent years.

CHAPTER 3

Is the Death Penalty Applied Fairly?

Overview: Death Penalty Demographics

Tracy L. Snell

Tracy L. Snell is a statistician for the Bureau of Justice Statistics within the US Department of Justice.

At year-end 2012, 35 states and the Federal Bureau of Prisons held 3,033 inmates under sentence of death, which was 32 fewer than at year-end 2011. This represents the twelfth consecutive year in which the number of inmates under sentence of death decreased.

Prisoners with Death Sentences

Four states (California, Florida, Texas, and Pennsylvania) held more than half of all inmates on death row on December 31, 2012. The Federal Bureau of Prisons held 56 inmates under sentence of death at year-end 2012.

Of prisoners under sentence of death at year-end 2012, 56% were white and 42% were black. The 384 Hispanic inmates under sentence of death accounted for 14% of inmates with a known ethnicity. Ninety-eight percent of inmates under sentence of death were male, and 2% were female. The race and sex of inmates under sentence of death has remained relatively unchanged since 2000.

Among inmates for whom legal status at the time of the capital offense was available, 40% had an active criminal justice status. About 4 in 10 of these inmates were on parole, and nearly 3 in 10 were on probation. The remaining inmates had charges pending, were incarcerated, had escaped from incarceration, or had some other criminal justice status.

Tracy L. Snell, "Capital Punishment, 2012—Statistical Tables," Bureau of Justice Statistics, no. NCJ 245789, May, 2014, pp. 1–2.

Criminal history patterns of death row inmates differed by race and Hispanic origin. More black inmates had a prior felony conviction (73%), compared to Hispanic (64%) or white (63%) inmates. Similar percentages of white (9%), black (9%), and Hispanic (6%) inmates had a prior homicide conviction. A slightly higher percentage of Hispanic (32%) and black (30%) inmates were on probation or parole at the time of their capital offense, compared to 24% of white inmates.

The Death Penalty in 2012

In 2012, 19 states and the Federal Bureau of Prisons reported that 79 inmates were received under sentence of death. Admissions in Florida (20), California (13), Texas (9), and Pennsylvania (6) accounted for 61% of those sentenced to death in 2012.

The number of inmates received in 2012 was the smallest number of admissions to death row since 1973 when 44 persons were admitted.

Twenty states and the Federal Bureau of Prisons removed 111 inmates from under sentence of death: 43 were executed, 17 died by means other than execution, and 51 were removed as a result of commutations or courts overturning sentences or convictions. Removals in Texas (17) and Florida (10) accounted for a quarter of all inmates removed from under sentence of death in 2012.

Nine states executed 43 inmates in 2012. The inmates executed in 2012 had been under sentence of death an average of 15 years and 10 months, which was 8 months less than those executed in 2011.

Among the 36 jurisdictions with prisoners under sentence of death at year-end 2012, 5 jurisdictions had more inmates than at year-end 2011, 13 had fewer inmates, and 18 had the same number. Florida showed the largest increase (up 10 inmates). Oklahoma and Texas (down 8 each), followed by Mississippi (down 7), North Carolina (down 6), and Arizona (down 5) had the largest decreases.

The Death Penalty in Recent Decades

The U.S. Supreme Court reinstated the death penalty in 1976. From 1976 to 2000, the number of inmates under sentence of death in the U.S. steadily increased until it peaked at 3,601 inmates on December 31, 2000. In 2001, the number of inmates removed from under sentence of death was higher than the number admitted for the first time since 1976. The number of annual removals of those under sentence of death exceeded the number of admissions every year since 2001. The 79 inmates received under sentence of death in 2012 represent a 5% decrease from the 83 inmates received in 2011. The number of inmates received in 2012 was the smallest number of admissions to death row since 1973 when 44 persons were admitted.

Of the 8,032 people under sentence of death between 1977 and 2012, 16% had been executed, 6% died by causes other than execution, and 40% received other dispositions. The federal government began collecting annual execution statistics in 1930. Between 1930 and 2012, a total of 5,179 inmates were executed under civil authority. After the Supreme Court reinstated death penalty statutes in 1976, 35 states and the federal government executed 1,320 inmates.

Disparity in Death Penalty Rates Is Not Evidence of Racial Bias

Kent S. Scheidegger

Kent S. Scheidegger is the legal director of the Criminal Justice Legal Foundation.

Opponents of the death penalty speak breathlessly of "disparities" in the application of the death penalty. In its broadest sense, "disparity" simply means that someone compiled some numbers and found that some rate differs among ethnic groups or among localities. Of course rates differ. The country and the state are heterogeneous. Crime rates vary. The extent to which witnesses are willing to come forward varies. Many factors vary. A mere difference in raw data is not proof that invidious racial discrimination is the cause of the difference. It should not even be considered as evidence of such discrimination. Disparity is evidence of discrimination only when a careful analysis of cases rules out legitimate reasons for the difference. . . .

The word "discriminate" has negative connotations from its association with racial discrimination, but in its core meaning "discriminate" simply means "To make a clear distinction; distinguish. . . . To make sensible decisions; judge wisely." The Supreme Court's requirement of individualized sentencing is a requirement that sentencers "discriminate" on the basis of legitimate factors that distinguish the more culpable murderers from those that are less so. When the legitimate factors happen to correlate with illegitimate factors, the raw data on demographics tell us nothing.

Studies in this area attempt to cope with this problem by examining case files for the legitimate factors and developing mathematical models to adjust for them. The problem is that the legitimate factors cannot be fully known from the case files, and the studies never include all the legitimate factors even when they are discernable. For example, the model from the Baldus Georgia study primarily used by the petitioner in the *McCleskey* case was held to be invalid by the Federal District Court because (among other deficiencies) it failed to account for the strength of the prosecution's case for guilt. Prosecutors certainly should be more reluctant to seek the death penalty when the case for guilt is less than airtight, and juries certainly should be more reluctant to impose it when they have lingering doubt. . . .

The Race of the Defendant

By far, the type of potential discrimination of greatest concern is discrimination against racial minority defendants on the basis of their race. This form alone, of all the disparities commonly discussed, would, if true, mean that people are on death row who do not deserve to be there. (The others are discussed below.) Discrimination against black defendants was the great concern looming in the background when the Supreme Court threw out the then-existing death penalty laws in 1972 [in *Furman v. Georgia*].

Fortunately, nearly all the studies of post-1972 capital sentencing show no evidence of race-of-defendant bias. This result is particularly striking given that many of the studies are conducted or sponsored by opponents of capital punishment for the specific purpose of attacking it. While a study result that supports a sponsor's argument should be regarded with suspicion, a result that contradicts the sponsor's argument conversely warrants special confidence. The authors [David C.

Baldus, Charles Pulaski, and George Woodworth] of the best known of these studies, the Baldus study in Georgia, noted, "What is most striking about these results is the total absence of any race-of-defendant effect." This result has been repeated many times in many jurisdictions, including New Jersey, Maryland, Nebraska, Virginia, and the federal system. As in any field of study, there are some outliers. Overall, though, this result is sufficiently consistent that even a prominent death penalty opponent [Virginia Sloan] concedes, "It's not the race of the defendant that is the major factor, and I don't think there are many studies that claim that."

"Disparity" is not a defect; it is a virtue.

The result in Connecticut follows the national pattern. A study commissioned by an opponent—the Public Defender—concluded flatly, "There was no evidence that the defendant's race was related to procedural and sentencing advancement." Decades of the most strenuous searching for race-of-defendant bias in the post-1972 era has come up empty. This is a success to be celebrated. The post-*Furman* reforms worked.

With the most salient form of discrimination unsupported by their own studies, opponents of the death penalty turned to more esoteric forms. These include the claimed "race-of-victim bias" and "geographic disparity." We will take them in reverse order, because it is necessary to understand the geographic effect in order to understand the true cause of the numbers claimed to support "race-of-victim bias."

The Charge of Geographic "Disparity"

In America, government power and decision making are divided among many levels and many independent branches of government, more so than in any other country. This division is by design, not by accident, and it is an essential part of the genius of the American system. Indeed, one of the reasons we still have the death penalty in most of the United States, while elitists have repealed it over the objections of the people in many other countries, is because our divided-power structure keeps the government more responsive to the wishes of the people.

The fundamental question of whether the death penalty will be an available option for murder is decided at the state level. For the worst murders, the death penalty is available in Connecticut and New Hampshire but not in Massachusetts or Vermont. This is a "geographic disparity." This is also American federal democracy working as designed. The people of each of these states have chosen to have or not have the death penalty through the democratic process. The same is true of noncapital sentencing. The decision of how many years in prison are sufficient to punish rape, for example, is one the people of each state can make for themselves. "Disparity" is not a defect; it is a virtue.

The actual implementation of the criminal law is, to a large extent, delegated further down to the local level. In almost every state, prosecutors are elected by county or local district. Even more importantly, juries are selected locally. A jury of the "vicinage" is considered an important component of the constitutional right of trial by jury. The jury is expected to represent the "conscience of the community," not the conscience of the state.

When decisions are made that involve the exercise of discretion, different people will necessarily make different decisions in some cases, particularly the close cases. Local selection of decision-makers necessarily results in variation among localities. This happens all the time in noncapital cases. If a homicide is on the ragged edge between murder and manslaughter, a prosecutor in one jurisdiction may offer a plea bargain to manslaughter that would not be offered in another, or juries in the two localities might come in with different verdicts after trial of similar cases. There is no wailing and gnashing of teeth over these variations in noncapital cases. They are an understood and accepted product of local control.

Even if the claim [of racial bias] were valid, then, it would not be an argument for doing away with the death penalty.

The death penalty is for the worst murders and murderers, but "worst" cannot be mechanically defined. Distinguishing the worst from the not-quite-worst is necessarily a matter of discretion. We should not be surprised if an urban community jaded by chronic violence defines the worst murders more restrictively than a community where violence is comparatively rare. As with other "geographic disparities," this is not a defect; it is local control working as designed. Among the most thorough analyses in this area is by Judge David Baime, appointed as a special master by the Supreme Court of New Jersey. What he concluded could just as easily be said of Connecticut:

> New Jersey is a small and densely populated state. It is, nevertheless, a heterogenous one. It is thus not remarkable that the counties do not march in lockstep in the manner in which death-eligible cases are prosecuted.

The 2003 Connecticut Study proceeds on the premise that geographic variation is judicially suspect. That is a fundamentally erroneous premise. Geographic variation is a normal and proper product of local elections and juries of the vicinage in the American criminal justice system.

The Race of the Victim

Ever since the Baldus study in Georgia in the 1980s, the primary discrimination claim has been that the death penalty is imposed less often when the victim is black. Even if that were true, it would not mean that a single person is on death row who does not deserve to be there. The race-neutral benchmark for which cases deserve the death penalty is set in cases where race is not a factor, *i.e.*, where the perpetrator, victim, and principal decision-makers are all the same race. In practice, in most of American society traditionally, that has meant when they are all white. If the death penalty is imposed less often when the victim is black, that means that there are perpetrators in black-victim cases who should have been sentenced to death but were not. The unjustly lenient sentences in such a hypothetical case cannot, in any event, be corrected with unjust leniency in another case. Even if the claim were valid, then, it would not be an argument for doing away with the death penalty. It would be an argument for redoubling efforts to obtain death sentences in black-victim cases where the sentence is warranted.

When murder is more common, people tend to become jaded and less easily shocked.

The claim is not valid, though. Time after time, when the data are properly analyzed and confounding factors properly controlled, the claimed race-of-victim bias has vanished into the statistical grass. . . .

The federal system has been the subject of a unique research effort in this regard. A release of raw data in 2000, making no attempt to control for legitimate case characteristics, had raised charges that there was a race-of-victim bias in the Department of Justice's decision to seek the death penalty. Following the gathering of data needed for proper controls, the analysis was assigned to three independent teams to determine whether the data really did indicate racial bias. The three independent teams came to consistent conclusions: "The disparities disappear when data in the AG's [Attorny General] case files are used to adjust for the heinousness of the crime."

Results of studies from other states are mostly consistent with the federal result. In California, a study by RAND Corporation found no evidence of discrimination based on either the race of the victim or the race of the defendant. In Nebraska, Baldus *et al.* found "no significant evidence of systemic disparate treatment on the basis of the race of the defendant or the race of the victim in either the major urban counties or the counties of greater Nebraska on the part of either the prosecutors or judges." In Maryland, when the apparent race-of-victim effect was controlled for jurisdiction, it disappeared at some points in the study, but a residual effect remained at other points.

The 2003 study in Connecticut is consistent with these results. As noted previously, there is no evidence of a race-of-defendant bias. The study found a relation between race of the victim and the intermediate step of proceeding to a penalty trial, but none with the important final result of a death sentence. The needed correction for the legitimate variable of jurisdiction could not be done because the sample size was too small. The information available therefore provides no reason to doubt that the situation in Connecticut is consistent with the overall national picture, *i.e.*, that claimed racial disparities would shrink to insignificance if legitimate factors, *including jurisdiction*, could properly be taken into account. . . .

The False Impression of Racial Bias

Why is it that more sparing use of the death penalty by jurisdiction correlates with race, such that statewide numbers give a false impression of racial bias that dissipates upon proper correction for jurisdiction? There are two obvious reasons. The first is the unpleasant but undeniable reality in America today that the urban centers with high black populations also tend to have higher crime rates and particularly higher murder rates. . . . When murder is more common, people tend to become jaded and less easily shocked.

The second reason is that opposition to capital punishment is much higher among black Americans than among any other demographic group. Over the past several decades, white Americans have favored the death penalty by overwhelming margins. Solid majorities are in favor among both Republicans and Democrats, both college graduates and those with high school or less, both young and old, and even liberals and conservatives. Black Americans alone, among all the groups tallied, have been about evenly divided, with relatively narrow majorities shifting between support and opposition.

What happens when a demographic group with unusually strong opposition to the death penalty comprises an unusually large proportion of the population in a particular locality? Charles Lane of the *Washington Post* notes,

> In jurisdictions with large African-American populations, where most black-on-black crime occurs, persuading a jury to sentence the defendant to death is relatively difficult. . . . Also, in jurisdictions where elected prosecutors must appeal to black voters, prosecutors are that much less likely to support capital punishment.
>
> This is how race-of-the-victim disparities can be said to reflect racial progress. After all, blacks neither voted in elections nor served on juries in substantial numbers, especially in the South, until the late 1960s. Now that they do, they appear to be using this power to limit capital punishment in the cases closest to them.

The NAACP's [National Association for the Advancement of Colored People] statement to the Judiciary Committee claims, "Statistics show time and again that the color of skin of victims is one of the most telling indicators of whether or not someone will get a death sentence." That is simply not true. What the statistics show, when properly analyzed, is that the NAACP and other opponents of the death penalty have succeeded in reducing the application of the death penalty within the communities with the highest black populations and the greatest numbers of black-victim murders.

For those of us who believe that the death penalty is appropriate for the worst murderers, this is not a good result. It is not, however, a product or an indication of racism.

In summary, there is no good reason to believe the claim that race is a predominant factor, or even a major factor, in determining which murderers are sentenced to death. What limited disparities may remain are not even close to a sufficient reason to abandon justice and settle for an inadequate, watered-down sentence for the worst murderers, whatever color they may be.

Justice After Troy Davis

Ross Douthat

Ross Douthat is an op-ed columnist for The New York Times.

It's easy to see why the case of Troy Davis, the Georgia man executed last week [September 21, 2011] for the 1989 killing of an off-duty police officer, became a cause célèbre for death penalty opponents. Davis was identified as the shooter by witnesses who later claimed to have been coerced by investigators. He was prosecuted and convicted based on the same dubious eyewitness testimony, rather than forensic evidence. And his appeals process managed to be ponderously slow without delivering anything like certainty: it took the courts 20 years to say a final no to the second trial that Davis may well have deserved.

The Concern About Innocence

For many observers, the lesson of this case is simple: We need to abolish the death penalty outright. The argument that capital punishment is inherently immoral has long been a losing one in American politics. But in the age of DNA evidence and endless media excavations, the argument that courts and juries are just too fallible to be trusted with matters of life and death may prove more effective.

If capital punishment disappears in the United States, it won't be because voters and politicians no longer want to execute the guilty. It will be because they're afraid of executing the innocent.

This is a healthy fear for a society to have. But there's a danger here for advocates of criminal justice reform. After all, in a world without the death penalty, Davis probably wouldn't have been retried or exonerated. His appeals would still have been denied, he would have spent the rest of his life in prison, and far fewer people would have known or cared about his fate.

The Importance of Scrutiny

Instead, he received a level of legal assistance, media attention and activist support that few convicts can ever hope for. And his case became an example of how the very finality of the death penalty can focus the public's attention on issues that many Americans prefer to ignore: the overzealousness of cops and prosecutors, the limits of the appeals process and the ugly conditions faced by many of the more than two million Americans currently behind bars.

The case for executing murderers is a case for proportionality in punishment: for sentences that fit the crime, and penalties that close the circle.

Simply throwing up our hands and eliminating executions entirely, by contrast, could prove to be a form of moral evasion—a way to console ourselves with the knowledge that no innocents are ever executed, even as more pervasive abuses go unchecked. We should want a judicial system that we can trust with matters of life and death, and that can stand up to the kind of public scrutiny that Davis's case received. And gradually reforming the death penalty—imposing it in fewer situations and with more safeguards, which other defendants could benefit from as well—might do more than outright abolition to address the larger problems with crime and punishment in America.

This point was made well last week by Pascal-Emmanuel Gobry, writing for *The American Scene*. In any penal system, he pointed out, but especially in our own—which can be brutal, overcrowded, rife with rape and other forms of violence—a lifelong prison sentence can prove more cruel and unusual than a speedy execution. And a society that supposedly values liberty as much or more than life itself hasn't necessarily become more civilized if it preserves its convicts' lives while consistently violating their rights and dignity. It's just become better at self-deception about what's really going on.

The Need for Genuine Justice

Fundamentally, most Americans who support the death penalty do so because they want to believe that our justice system is *just*, and not merely a mechanism for quarantining the dangerous in order to keep the law-abiding safe. The case for executing murderers is a case for proportionality in punishment: for sentences that fit the crime, and penalties that close the circle.

Instead of dismissing this point of view as backward and barbaric, criminal justice reformers should try to harness it, by pointing out that too often our punishments don't fit the crime—that sentences for many drug crimes are disproportionate to the offenses, for instance, or that rape and sexual assault have become an implicit part of many prison terms. Americans should be urged to support penal reform not in spite of their belief that some murderers deserve execution, in other words, but because of it—because both are attempts to ensure that accused criminals receive their just deserts.

Abolishing capital punishment in a kind of despair over its fallibility would send a very different message. It would tell the public that our laws and courts and juries are fundamentally incapable of delivering what most Americans consider genuine justice. It could encourage a more cynical and utilitarian view of why police forces and prisons exist, and what moral standards we should hold them to. And while it would put an end to wrongful executions, it might well lead to more overall injustice.

The US Death Penalty Is Inseparable from White Supremacy

Ta-Nehisi Coates

Ta-Nehisi Coates is a senior editor for The Atlantic.

Fifteen years ago, Clayton Lockett shot Stephanie Neiman twice, then watched as his friends buried her alive. Last week [April 29, 2014], Lockett was tortured to death by the state of Oklahoma. The torture was not so much the result of intention as neglect. The state knew that its chosen methods—a triple-drug cocktail—could result in a painful death. (An inmate executed earlier this year by the method was heard to say, "I feel my whole body burning.") Oklahoma couldn't care less. It executed Lockett anyway.

The Issue of Racial Bias

Over at *Bloomberg View*, Ramesh Ponnuru has taken the occasion to pen a column ostensibly arguing against the death penalty. But Ponnuru, evidently embarrassed to find himself in liberal company, spends most of the column dismissing the arguments of soft-headed bedfellows:

> On the core issue—yes or no on capital punishment—I'm with the opponents. Better to err on the side of not taking life. The teaching of the Catholic Church, to which I belong, seems right to me: The state has the legitimate authority to execute criminals, but it should refrain if it has other means of protecting people from them. Our government almost always does.

Still, when I hear about an especially gruesome crime, like the one the Oklahoma killer committed, I can't help rooting for the death penalty. And a lot of the arguments its opponents make are unconvincing.

Take the claims of racial bias—that we execute black killers, or the killers of white victims, at disproportionate rates. Even if those disputed claims are true, they don't point toward abolition of the death penalty. Executing more white killers, or killers of black victims, would reduce any disparity just as well.

Well into the 20th century, capital punishment was, as John Locke would say, lynching "coloured with the name, pretences, or forms of law."

Indeed it would. But the reason we don't do this is contained within Ponnuru's inquiry: bias. When Ponnuru suggests that the way to correct for the death penalty's disproportionate use is to execute more white people, he is presenting a world in which the death penalty has neither history nor context. One merely flips the "Hey Guys, Let's Not Be Racist" switch and then the magic happens.

The History of White Supremacy

Those of us who cite the disproportionate application of the death penalty as a reason for outlawing it do so because we believe that a criminal-justice system is not an abstraction but a real thing, existing in a real context, with a real history. In America, the history of the criminal justice—and the death penalty—is utterly inseparable from white supremacy. During the Civil War, black soldiers were significantly more likely to be court-martialed and executed than their white counterparts. This practice continued into World War II. "African-Americans comprised 10 percent of the armed forces but accounted for almost 80 percent of the soldiers executed during the war," writes law professor Elizabeth Lutes Hillman.

In American imagination, the lynching era is generally seen as separate from capital punishment. But virtually no one was ever charged for lynching. The country refused to outlaw it. And sitting U.S. senators such as Ben Tillman and Theodore Bilbo openly called for lynching for crimes as grave as rape and as dubious as voting. Well into the 20th century, capital punishment was, as John Locke would say, lynching "coloured with the name, pretences, or forms of law."

The youngest American ever subjected to the death penalty was George Junius Stinney. It is very hard to distinguish his case from an actual lynching. At age 14, Stinney, a black boy, walked to the execution chamber

> with a Bible under his arm, which he later used as a booster seat in the electric chair. Standing 5 foot 2 inches (157 cm) tall and weighing just over 90 pounds (40 kg), his size (relative to the fully grown prisoners) presented difficulties in securing him to the frame holding the electrodes. Nor did the state's adult-sized face-mask fit him; as he was hit with the first 2,400 V surge of electricity, the mask covering his face slipped off, "revealing his wide-open, tearful eyes and saliva coming from his mouth. . . . After two more jolts of electricity, the boy was dead."

Living with racism in America means tolerating a level of violence inflicted on the black body that we would not upon the white body. This deviation is not a random fact, but the price of living in a society with a lengthy history of considering black people as a lesser strain of humanity. When you live in such a society, the prospect of incarcerating, disenfranchising, and ultimately executing white humans at the same rate as black humans makes makes very little sense. Disproportion is the point.

A Disturbing Logic

The "Hey Guys, Let's Not Be Racist" switch is really "Hey Guys, Let's Pretend We Aren't American" switch or a "Hey

Guys, Let's Pretend We Aren't Human Beings" switch. The death penalty—like all state actions—exists within a context constructed by humans, not gods. Humans tend to have biases, and the systems we construct often reflect those biases. Understanding this, it is worth asking whether our legal system should be in the business of doling out an ultimate punishment, one for which there can never be any correction. Citing racism in our justice system isn't mere shaming, it's a call for a humility and self-awareness, which presently evades us.

I was sad to see Ponnuru's formulation, because it so echoed the unfortunate thoughts of William F. Buckley. In 1965, Buckley debated James Baldwin at the Cambridge Union Society. That was the year John Lewis was beaten at the Edmund Pettus Bridge, and Viola Liuzzo was shot down just outside of Selma, Alabama. In that same campaign, Martin Luther King gave, arguably, his greatest speech. ("How Long? Not long. Truth forever on the scaffold. Wrong forever on the throne.") In whole swaths of the country, black people lacked the basic rights of citizenship—central among them, the right to vote. Buckley spent much of his time sneering at complaints of American racism. When the issue of the vote was raised Buckley responded by saying that the problem with Mississippi wasn't that "not enough Negroes have the vote but that too many white people are voting."

There's something revealed in the logic—in both Ponnuru and Buckley's case—that we should fix disproportion by making more white people into niggers. It is the same logic of voter-ID laws, which will surely disenfranchise huge swaths of white voters, for the goal of disenfranchising proportionally more black voters. I'm not sure what all that means—it's the shadow of something I haven't worked out.

The Death Penalty Is Carried Out Against Those with Mental Illness

Natasha Lennard

Natasha Lennard is a senior news analyst for Vice News.

In December 2008, Andre Thomas pulled out and ate his left eyeball. He had gouged out the right eye in 2004, having taken a bible passage literally, six days after he brutally murdered his estranged wife, their young son and her 13-month-old daughter. His attorney Maurie Levin, who is co-director of Texas' Capital Punishment Clinic, told *Salon* that her client is "transparently and floridly" mentally ill. He was diagnosed as schizophrenic while in prison, having heard voices in his head since childhood. What sort of system sentences Andre Thomas to death?

Mental Illness and Criminal Justice

Texas Tribune managing editor Brandi Grissom has followed Thomas' case closely. As she noted in an excellent feature for the *Texas Monthly*, "as he awaits execution, Andre and his tragic case force uncomfortable questions about the intersection of mental illness and the criminal justice system." Thomas is certainly not the only death row inmate to have been diagnosed with mental illness; more than 20 percent of the 290 inmates on Texas' death row are considered mentally ill, as Grissom noted. But the extremity of his situation has prompted fervid responses locally and nationally. "It's astonishing, just how many problems in the legal system [this case] exemplifies," said Levin in a phone interview.

Natasha Lennard, "A Schizophrenic Who Gouged Out His Eyes Is on Texas Death Row," February 25, 2013. This article first appeared in Salon.com, at http://www.Salon.com. An online version remains in the Salon archives. Reprinted with permission.

Who gets to be sane? Who gets to be accountable? Who gets to be executed?—Thomas, fully blind and heavily medicated, faces the death penalty as a limit case for Texas' answer to these problematic questions.

[Thomas] was deemed competent to stand trial—trial for capital murder at that—after he had already gouged out his eye and exhibited other psychotic tendencies.

To be sure, the crime for which Thomas was capitally charged was horrific. Grissom's account bears reprinting:

By 2004, Andre was 21 years old, deeply mentally ill, and receiving no treatment. On the bright, clear morning of March 27, he charged up the stairs to the third-floor apartment where Laura [his estranged wife] lived and kicked in the door. Her boyfriend had already left for work. Andre was holding three knives, one for each of his intended victims. He first encountered Laura, who ran toward him, screaming "No!" Andre plunged a knife into her chest. He then reached in and pulled out what he believed was her heart (he had, in fact, extracted part of her lung). Next, he headed for the children's room, where Andre Jr. and 1-year-old Leyha were sleeping. Andre held down his 4-year-old son and stabbed him before moving on to Leyha. He carved out each of the children's hearts. Finally, Andre jammed a knife into his own chest three times and lay down beside Laura on the living room floor, expecting to die. Confounded when he didn't, he slipped the organs he had removed into his pocket and walked more than five miles home. A few hours later, he went to the Sherman Police Department, where he confessed to the murders and asked if he would be forgiven. "I thought it was what God wanted me to do," he later told investigators.

After undergoing emergency surgery to repair his life-threatening stab wounds, Andre was moved to the Grayson County jail, where his behavior became more and more psychotic. He gestured wildly and announced that he was going to save the world. He claimed to be "the thirteenth warrior on the dollar bill" and said that Laura and the children weren't dead but that their hearts had been freed from evil.

There is no correct procedure to deal with Andre Thomas. The questions of how someone ends up in such a tormented state—the conditions that make the above horrors possible—are far beyond the purview of this writing. We can say, however, that there are many profoundly wrong ways to deal with Andre Thomas—and these are the ways he has been dealt with.

The idea of justice at play here rests on a person being able to understand, in advance of their execution, why and for what they are being killed.

Problems in the Case

Firstly, he was deemed competent to stand trial—trial for capital murder at that—after he had already gouged out his eye and exhibited other psychotic tendencies. While considered competent to be tried for a death sentence, it's worth noting that the Texas Department of Criminal Justice deemed him incompetent to speak with a journalist. As Grissom wrote, while she was permitted to tour the psychiatric facility currently holding Thomas, [she] was not allowed to speak with him. "John Hurt, a spokesman for the department, explained that the policy is meant to protect inmates 'who may not be mentally competent to sit for an interview.' It was a remarkable response given that Andre had already been deemed competent for trial and is currently considered competent to be executed," wrote Grissom.

But this is just one of many paradoxes and absurdities characterizing Thomas' treatment—among them the fact that the Texas Court of Criminal Appeals found the defendant "clearly 'crazy' but . . . also 'sane' under Texas law."

Undergirding the case is the problem of racism in the criminal justice system. Thomas, a young African American man in a small town in Texas was tried in front of an all white jury for the murder of a white woman. Four jurors, Levin told *Salon*, had written on a questionnaire that they objected to interracial relationships. According to the attorney and legal scholar, the prosecutor went on a "soliloquy ... invoking race based fears" about the defendant "getting out and dating your daughters."

Thomas was sentenced to death and—like all those so condemned—was confined to a six-by-10 ft. cell for 23 hours a day. The facility, says Levin, showed "shocking inadequacy" in dealing with Thomas' mental deterioration. There, the convicted man gouged out his other eye and rendered himself fully blind. Thomas and his legal team currently await the decision of a federal court on whether he is sane enough to be executed.

As a limit case, Thomas highlights the juridical determinations around the right to life: What are the conditions necessary for the state to kill a person? The arguments in Thomas' first capital murder trial fell around whether the killer knew right from wrong at the time of carrying out the murders. Now, the terrain of debate has shifted to whether Thomas is competent enough to comprehend his own capital punishment. Levin argues that her client lacks any such rational understanding and that, although treated with anti-psychotic medicines, he still hears voices, she said.

The Legal Framework

The entire legal framework is troubling. The idea of justice at play here rests on a person being able to understand, in advance of their execution, why and for what they are being killed. Grissom cites Thurgood Marshall's 1986 majority SCOTUS [Supreme Court of the United States] opinion on the issue of executing the mentally ill, which set up the current legal standard: "We may seriously question the retributive value of executing a person who has no comprehension of why he has been singled out and stripped of his fundamental right to life," wrote Justice Marshall. While, of course, many of us would also vehemently challenge the retributive value of the state executing persons with full comprehension of why they have been so singled out to face death, it seems clear that Marshall's "comprehension" condition sets up profound problems when it comes to the mentally ill.

When it comes to the intellectually disabled (referred to in U.S. law as "mentally retarded") the story is slightly different. The Supreme Court has ruled that the "mentally retarded," as well as juveniles, cannot be held to the same standards of culpability as most adults and thus the death penalty in such cases would violate the constitution's ban on cruel and unusual punishment. Of course, even in cases of proven mental disability, death sentences are still carried out. The state of Georgia, for example, is currently pushing to have a stay of execution removed in the case of 38-year-old Warren Hill, a death row inmate found mentally retarded by physicians. Mental illness—where there is sometimes possibility of medicating a prisoner into a state of execution-worthy comprehension—brings up even more troubling grey areas for capital sentencing.

Levin told *Salon* that there is a "deficit in forums to even discuss how to redress the issues this case raises." If the case of Andre Thomas—schizophrenic, self-blinded and facing death by the state—doesn't urge the importance of such forums, it's hard to imagine what might.

Innocent People Are Given Death Sentences

Samuel R. Gross et al.

Samuel R. Gross coauthored the following viewpoint with Barbara O'Brien, Chen Hu, and Edward H. Kennedy. Gross is the Thomas and Mabel Long Professor of Law at the University of Michigan Law School. O'Brien is associate professor of law at Michigan State University College of Law. Hu and Kennedy are biostatisticians at the American College of Radiology Clinical Research Center and the University of Pennsylvania School of Medicine, respectively.

In the past few decades a surge of hundreds of exonerations of innocent criminal defendants has drawn attention to the problem of erroneous conviction, and led to a spate of reforms in criminal investigation and adjudication. All the same, the most basic empirical question about false convictions remains unanswered: How common are these miscarriages of justice?

Estimating False Convictions

False convictions, by definition, are unobserved when they occur: If we know that a defendant is innocent, he is not convicted in the first place. They are also extremely difficult to detect after the fact. As a result, the great majority of innocent defendants remain undetected. The rate of such errors is often described as a "dark figure"—an important measure of the performance of the criminal justice system that is not merely unknown but unknowable.

However, there is no shortage of lawyers and judges who assert confidently that the number of false convictions is negligible. Judge Learned Hand said so in 1923: "Our [criminal] procedure has always been haunted by the ghost of the innocent man convicted. It is an unreal dream." And in 2007, Justice Antonin Scalia wrote in a concurring opinion in the Supreme Court that American criminal convictions have an "error rate of [0].027 percent—or, to put it another way, a success rate of 99.973 percent." This would be comforting, if true. In fact, the claim is silly. Scalia's ratio is derived by taking the number of known exonerations at the time, which were limited almost entirely to a small subset of murder and rape cases, using it as a measure of all false convictions (known and unknown), and dividing it by the number of all felony convictions for all crimes, from drug possession and burglary to car theft and income tax evasion.

The vast majority of criminal convictions are not candidates for exoneration because no one makes any effort to reconsider the guilt of the defendants.

To actually estimate the proportion of erroneous convictions we need a well-defined group of criminal convictions within which we identify all mistaken convictions, or at least most. It is hard to imagine how that could be done for criminal convictions generally, but it might be possible for capital murder.

The Exoneration Rate

The rate of exonerations among death sentences in the United States is far higher than for any other category of criminal convictions. Death sentences represent less than one-tenth of 1% of prison sentences in the United States, but they accounted for about 12% of known exonerations of innocent defendants from 1989 through early 2012, a disproportion of more than 130 to 1. A major reason for this extraordinary exoneration rate is that far more attention and resources are devoted to death penalty cases than to other criminal prosecutions, before and after conviction.

The vast majority of criminal convictions are not candidates for exoneration because no one makes any effort to reconsider the guilt of the defendants. Approximately 95% of felony convictions in the United States are based on negotiated pleas of guilty (plea bargains) that are entered in routine proceedings at which no evidence is presented. Few are ever subject to any review whatsoever. Most convicted defendants are never represented by an attorney after conviction, and the appeals that do take place are usually perfunctory and unrelated to guilt or innocence.

The proportion of death-sentenced inmates who are exonerated understates the rate of false convictions among death sentences because the intensive search for possible errors is largely abandoned once the threat of execution is removed.

Death sentences are different. Almost all are based on convictions after jury trial, and even the handful of capital defendants who plead guilty are then subject to trial-like-sentencing hearings, usually before juries. All death sentences are reviewed on appeal; almost all are reviewed repeatedly. With few exceptions, capital defendants have lawyers as long as they remain on death row. Everyone, from the first officer on the scene of a potentially capital crime to the Chief Justice of the United States, takes capital cases more seriously than other criminal prosecutions—and knows that everybody else will do so as well. And everyone from defense lawyers to innocence projects to governors and state and federal judges is likely to be particularly careful to avoid the execution of innocent defendants.

This extraordinary difference in resources and attention generates two related effects. (*i*) Advocates for a defendant are much more likely to pursue any plausible postconviction claim of innocence if the defendant is under sentence of death. (*ii*) Courts (and other government actors) are much more likely to consider and grant such a claim if the defendant is at risk for execution. As a result, false convictions are far more likely to be detected among those cases that end in death sentences than in any other category of criminal convictions.

A Better Estimate

The high exoneration rate for death sentences suggests that a substantial proportion of innocent defendants who are sentenced to death are ultimately exonerated, perhaps a majority. If so, we can use capital exonerations as a basis for estimating a lower bound for the false conviction rate among death sentences.

Since 1973, when the first death penalty laws now in effect in the United States were enacted, 143 death-sentenced defendants have been exonerated, from 1 to 33 y after conviction (mean = 10.1 y). In a previous study we found that 2.3% of all death sentences imposed from 1973 through 1989 resulted in exoneration by the end of 2004. A study by [Michael] Risinger estimated that had biological samples been available for testing in all cases, 3.3% of defendants sentenced to death between 1982 and 1989 for murders that included rape would have been exonerated by DNA evidence through February 2006. That estimate, however, is based on a small number of exonerations ($n = 11$). Both studies were limited to convictions that occurred 15 y or more before the study date, and so include a high proportion of all exonerations that will ever occur in the relevant groups. Nonetheless both studies underestimate the false conviction rate for death-sentenced defendants because they do not reflect exonerations that occur after the study period, and do not include false convictions that are never detected at all.

Capital defendants who are removed from death row but not exonerated—typically because their sentences are reduced to life imprisonment—no longer receive the extraordinary level of attention that is devoted to death row inmates. (This applies as well to those who are executed or die on death row from other causes.) If they are in fact innocent, they are much less likely to be exonerated than if they had remained on death row. As a result, the proportion of death-sentenced inmates who are exonerated understates the rate of false convictions among death sentences because the intensive search for possible errors is largely abandoned once the threat of execution is removed.

In other words, the engine that produces an exoneration rate that is a plausible proxy for the rate of false conviction among death-sentenced prisoners is the process of reinvestigation and reconsideration under threat of execution. Over time, most death-sentenced inmates are removed from death row and resentenced to life in prison—at which point their chances of exoneration appear to drop back to the background rate for all murders, or close to it. Thus, we will get a better estimate of the rate of false capital convictions if [we] are able to estimate "what the rate of capital exonerations would be if all death sentences were subject for an indefinite period to the level of scrutiny that applies to those facing the prospect of execution." This study does just that. . . .

The Number of Innocents

We present a conservative estimate of the proportion of erroneous convictions of defendants sentenced to death in the United States from 1973 through 2004, 4.1%. This is a unique finding; there are no other reliable estimates of the rate of false conviction in any context. The main source of potential bias is the accuracy of our classification of cases as true or false convictions. On that issue it is likely that we have an undercount, that there are more innocent death row defendants who have not been identified and exonerated than guilty ones who have been exonerated in error.

The most charged question in this area is different: How many innocent defendants have been put to death? We cannot estimate that number directly but we believe it is comparatively low. If the rate were the same as our estimate for false death sentences, the number of innocents executed in the United States in the past 35 y would be more than 50. We do not believe that has happened. Our data and the experience of practitioners in the field both indicate that the criminal justice system goes to far greater lengths to avoid executing innocent defendants than to prevent them from remaining in prison indefinitely. One way to do so is to disproportionately reverse death sentences in capital cases in which the accuracy of the defendants' convictions is in doubt and to resentence them to life imprisonment, a practice that makes our estimate of the rate of error conservative. However, no process of removing potentially innocent defendants from the execution queue can be foolproof. With an error rate at trial over 4%, it is all but certain that several of the 1,320 defendants executed since 1977 were innocent.

Most innocent defendants who have been sentenced to death have not been exonerated, and many—including the great majority of those who have been resentenced to life in prison—probably never will be.

It is possible that the death-sentencing rate of innocent defendants has changed over time. No specific evidence points in that direction, but the number and the distribution of death sentences have changed dramatically in the past 15 y. One change, however, is unlikely to have much impact: the advent of DNA identification technology. DNA evidence is useful primarily in rape rather than homicide investigations. Only 13% of death row exonerations since 1973 (18 of 142) resulted from postconviction DNA testing, so the availability of preconviction testing will have at most a modest effect on that rate.

Unfortunately, we cannot generalize from our findings on death sentences to the rate of false convictions in any broader category of crime. Capital prosecutions, and to a lesser extent murder cases in general, are handled very differently from other criminal cases. There are theoretical reasons to believe that the rate of false conviction may be higher for murders in general, and for capital murders in particular, than for other felony convictions, primarily because the authorities are more likely to pursue difficult cases with weak evidence of guilt if one or more people have been killed. However, there are no data that confirm or refute this hypothesis.

We do know that the rate of error among death sentences is far greater than Justice Scalia's reassuring 0.027%. That much is apparent directly from the number of death row exonerations that have already occurred. Our research adds the disturbing news that most innocent defendants who have been sentenced to death have not been exonerated, and many—including the great majority of those who have been resentenced to life in prison—probably never will be.

This is only part of a disturbing picture. Fewer than half of all defendants who are convicted of capital murder are ever sentenced to death in the first place. Sentencing juries, like other participants in the process, worry about the execution of innocent defendants. Interviews with jurors who participated in capital sentencing proceedings indicate that lingering doubts about the defendant's guilt is the strongest available predictor of a sentence of life imprisonment rather than death. It follows that the rate of innocence must be higher for convicted capital defendants who are not sentenced to death than for those who are. The net result is that the great majority of innocent defendants who are convicted of capital murder in the

United States are neither executed nor exonerated. They are sentenced, or resentenced to prison for life, and then forgotten.

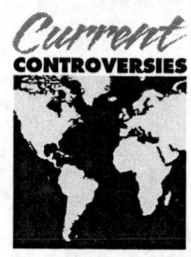

CHAPTER 4

How Should US Death Penalty Practices Be Reformed?

Overview: US Support for the Death Penalty

Pew Research Center

The Pew Research Center is a nonpartisan fact tank that informs the public about the issues, attitudes, and trends shaping America and the world.

According to a 2013 Pew Research Center survey, 55% of U.S. adults say they favor the death penalty for persons convicted of murder. A significant minority (37%) oppose the practice.

U.S. Support for the Death Penalty

While a majority of U.S. adults still support the death penalty, public opinion in favor of capital punishment has seen a modest decline since November 2011, the last time Pew Research asked the question. In 2011, fully six-in-ten U.S. adults (62%) favored the death penalty for murder convictions, and 31% opposed it.

Public support for capital punishment has ebbed and flowed over time, as indicated by polls going all the way back to the 1930s. But it has been gradually ticking downward for the past two decades, since Pew Research began collecting survey data on this issue. Since 1996, the margin between those who favor the death penalty and those who oppose it has narrowed from a 60-point gap (78% favor vs. 18% oppose) to an 18-point difference in 2013 (55% favor vs. 37% oppose).

Among most large U.S. religious groups, majorities support capital punishment. Roughly six-in-ten or more white evangelical Protestants (67%), white mainline Protestants (64%) and white Catholics (59%) express support for the death penalty.

By contrast, black Protestants are more likely to say they oppose the death penalty than support it (58% vs. 33%), as are Hispanic Catholics (54% vs. 37%).

Even among white adults, support for capital punishment has decreased markedly over the past two decades.

Support Across Demographic Groups

The differences among religious groups reflect the overall racial and ethnic picture on support for capital punishment. Twice as many white Americans favor the death penalty as oppose it (63% vs. 30%). Among black adults, the balance of opinion is reversed: 55% oppose capital punishment, while 36% support it. The margin is narrower among Hispanics, but more oppose the death penalty (50%) than support it (40%).

Even among white adults, support for capital punishment has decreased markedly over the past two decades, from 81% in 1996 to 63% in 2013. Over the same time period, the share of blacks favoring the death penalty also has declined, from 55% to 36%.

About half or more of most demographic groups support capital punishment, with only modest differences among them.

Men are slightly more likely than women to say they favor the death penalty (58% vs. 52%). And Americans ages 50 and older are more likely than those under 50 to support capital punishment, by a similar margin (58% vs. 53%).

Politically, the differences are somewhat greater. Fully seven-in-ten Republicans (71%) express support for the death penalty, while roughly a quarter (23%) oppose it. Among Democrats, public opinion is more evenly divided: 45% are in favor of the death penalty for convicted murderers, and 47%

are opposed. Political independents fall in between the two parties, with 57% supporting capital punishment and 37% opposing it.

The Death Penalty Should Be Replaced by Life Without Parole

Lauren Galik

Lauren Galik is director of criminal justice reform at the Reason Foundation.

Last month [April 2014] condemned Oklahoma death row inmate Clayton Lockett was pronounced dead from an apparent heart attack more than 40 minutes after his botched execution had begun.

During that time, horrified eyewitnesses watched as Lockett writhed on the gurney, gasped, and even spoke after doctors had declared him unconscious.

This bungled execution has breathed new life into the debate over the death penalty, prompting other states to examine their own protocols and question whether or not capital punishment is worth the costs. California should be no exception.

The Death Penalty in California

There are 746 inmates on death row in California. Since the death penalty was reinstated in 1978, California has only executed 13 inmates.

Roughly seven times more death row inmates have died from natural causes, suicide, or were killed in other ways than have actually been executed in California. Nevertheless, California taxpayers have paid more than $4 billion to have the death penalty in the state according to a study published in the 2011 *Loyola of Los Angeles Law Review*.

The last time California executed a prisoner was in 2006. That same year, a federal judge halted all executions in California on the grounds that the state's three-drug lethal injection protocol risked causing inmates too much pain and suffering before death, which would be a violation of the Eighth Amendment of the Constitution.

In 2013, a California state appeals court scrapped the state's attempt to update its lethal injection procedures and California's death penalty has remained in limbo ever since.

Everything about the death penalty is significantly more expensive.

It's not just California that has faced problems with its lethal injection protocol, essentially experimental drugs from unknown sources, resulting in a number of legal challenges over the constitutionality of these drugs and protocols.

The Costs of the Death Penalty

Meanwhile, housing prisoners on death row continues to cost California taxpayers $184 million more per year than it would if those same prisoners had been sentenced to life in prison without the possibility of parole.

That's because everything about the death penalty is significantly more expensive.

According to the *Loyola of Los Angeles Law Review* study, the heightened security practices mandated for death row inmates cost more than $100,000 per prisoner every year. The state also pays up to $300,000 for attorneys to represent each capital case inmate during his or her appeals process.

What's more—the least expensive death penalty trial in the history of the state still cost $1.1 million more than the most expensive case seeking life without parole.

A Better Alternative

It's true that the prisoners on death row in California are often the worst of the worst offenders and deserve the most severe punishment for their crimes.

However, eliminating the death penalty and requiring them to serve the rest of their lives in prison without the possibility of parole would still guarantee that they would die behind bars.

If California abolished the death penalty, taxpayers wouldn't have to keep wasting billions of dollars on death row. The state could also avoid the controversy and legal challenges that would accompany a change to its lethal injection protocol.

And citizens could rest easy knowing that no innocent person will accidentally be put to death.

According to a new study in the scientific journal *Proceedings of the National Academy of Sciences*, 4 percent of offenders on death row in the United States are innocent.

With worries over innocent people who could be killed by the state, botched executions, experimental lethal injection drugs and concerns over the cost and effectiveness of the death penalty, the time is right for California to get rid of capital punishment for good.

Life Without Parole Is a Different Kind of Death Sentence

David R. Dow

David R. Dow is the Cullen Professor at the University of Houston Law Center and has defended over one hundred death row inmates in the past twenty years.

If you were sentenced to life in prison with no chance of release, how long would you want to live? Would you want to live at all?

Inmates on Death Row

I think about these questions often. My clients, inmates on death row, think about them every day. In more than twenty years of representing prisoners facing execution, I've had several ask me to waive their appeals so they could hurry up and die. There are some who think any client who "volunteers"— that's our euphemism for giving up—is necessarily irrational. I don't share that view. To be sure, two of my clients who told me to waive their appeals were mentally ill, and I fought to keep them from volunteering to die. But the others were perfectly rational. They did not want to spend at least six years, maybe fifteen, appealing their sentences, only to ultimately be strapped to a gurney and injected with poison.

It's easy for most people to see their decisions as unhinged. We don't spend twenty-three hours a day in sixty-square-foot cells with no TV, limited access to radio, books or magazines, and no contact with other human beings (unless you count being escorted from point A to point B by often sadistic corrections officers). I've had clients who want me to fight for them, and then when we win and get their death sentence converted into life, end up telling me I've betrayed them.

Let me be clear: most of my clients want to live. Most of them prefer a life of virtually no freedom to no life at all. But underlying this preference is a hope, however faint, they might one day get out.

The Proposal to End Capital Punishment

On November 6 [2012], Californians will vote on Proposition 34, the Savings, Accountability and Full Enforcement (SAFE) for California Act. [The proposition was ultimately defeated.] The ballot initiative would abolish capital punishment in the state and replace it with a sentence of life in prison without the possibility of parole. Every week I get e-mails from national abolitionist groups touting the virtues of Prop 34. Facebook ads urge me to "like" it. But there are good reasons to believe that if the vote were up to the 725 inmates on California's death row, it would fail. When the Campaign to End the Death Penalty sent surveys on Prop 34 to more than 200 California death row prisoners, fifty inmates responded. Forty-seven opposed the measure.

Sending a prisoner to die behind bars with no hope of release is a sentence that denies the possibility of redemption every bit as much as strapping a murderer to the gurney and filling him with poison.

For California's 725 death row inmates, having their sentences commuted to life without parole would mean automatically losing their right to state-appointed lawyers to pursue their *habeas corpus* [right to appear in court] appeals. For a huge proportion, this would instantly rob them of every last ember of hope and increase by up to 20 percent the number of California inmates who will grow old and die behind bars. One California death row inmate recently wrote an op-ed opposing Prop 34 suggesting that he'd rather be executed than have his opportunities for appeal taken away. In a state that has executed only thirteen people since 1976, it would take two millennia to kill every current death row inmate, a fact that also helps explain how prisoners might oppose Prop 34.

Concerns over innocence seem to be at the heart of Prop 34. "California Leads the Nation in Wrongful Convictions," read a press release from the Yes on 34 campaign on October 24. "More Evidence that California Needs to Pass Prop 34 to Prevent Execution of an Innocent Person." Prop. 34 supporters point out that those with strong claims of innocence will still be entitled to receive court-appointed counsel. But few of the residents of death row will be able to make such a showing.

A Different Kind of Death Sentence

The justifications given by death penalty opponents who have embraced life without parole reveal the extent to which abolitionists have surrendered the moral basis of their position. It used to be that abolitionists argued that most people who commit bad acts can change and that the cruelest punishment one can inflict is to rob a human being of hope. But this concept—I hesitate to use the word "rehabilitation"—has seeped out of the criminal justice system over the past forty years. Prisons are now designed almost entirely for security in mind and not at all for socialization. Sentences have gotten steadily longer. And while states are turning away from the death penalty, they are replacing it with a different kind of death sentence. Sending a prisoner to die behind bars with no hope of release is a sentence that denies the possibility of redemption every bit as much as strapping a murderer to the gurney and filling him with poison.

Opponents of capital punishment often point out that the United States is the only developed Western country still executing prisoners, a comparison meant to shame us for being aligned with such human rights-violating countries as Iran, China and North Korea. It's not a bad argument, but exactly the same could be said about life without parole. Our neighbors to the south don't have it. Almost all of Europe rejects it. Even China and Pakistan, hardly exemplars of progressive criminal justice policy, allow prisoners serving life sentences to come up for parole after twenty-five years. Meanwhile, the United States imprisons wrongdoers for sentences that are five to seven times longer than sentences for comparable offenses in, say, Germany. Yet the recidivism rate in Germany is roughly 25 percent lower than ours.

> *There are scores, even hundreds [of prisoners], who could be released at no significant risk to society.*

Abolitionists might say in response that there are plenty of other reasons to support life without parole over the death penalty. It is less expensive, for example. This is true; carrying out an execution costs at least twice as much—and perhaps five times as much—as sentencing a murderer to life without parole. The Yes on 34 campaign argues that the measure would represent $130 million per year in savings for California.

Combined with the innocence argument—undeniably effective in a nation rattled by 300 DNA exonerations—this strategy seems to be working. Last year, a Gallup poll recorded the lowest level of support for the death penalty in forty years. Compared to a decade ago, when juries sentenced 224 criminals to death in a year, in 2011 American juries sent seventy-eight people to death row, the first time since 1976 that new arrivals on death row dipped below 100. Even in Texas—especially in Texas—which became the last death penalty state to adopt life without parole, in 2005, the decline in death sentences has been precipitous. In 1999, Texas juries added forty-eight inmates to death row. Last year's number was eight.

The Need for Permanent Sentencing

There's no question that touting life without parole as the moral and cost-effective alternative to the death penalty has been a successful short-term strategy. But then what? Is it really necessary to eliminate any possibility of eventual release for all 725 people on California's death row? Charles Manson is not serving life without parole, but he has been rejected every single time he has appeared before the parole board and will die behind bars. Are some of California's death row inmates as monstrous as Manson? I suspect the answer is yes, and the parole board could keep them in prison too. But there are scores, even hundreds, who could be released at no significant risk to society.

We know this because it has happened before. When the Supreme Court briefly struck down the death penalty in 1972, 587 men (and two women) had their death sentences instantly converted to life, and more than half of them were eventually paroled. Of the more than 300 who got out, five committed another homicide.

That's five deaths too many, you might say, and I would not disagree. But that's not really the question. The question is whether we need permanent sentencing to prevent such crimes. The question is how much safer we are by having a punishment that forecloses on any possibility for redemption. The question is whether any marginal increase in safety and savings are justified by the high cost of keeping aging inmates behind bars until they die.

This series of questions, you might have noticed, is exactly the same as the set one might ask in the face of capital punishment.

The Death Penalty Should Be Abolished

Marc Hyden

Marc Hyden is the national advocacy coordinator for Conservatives Concerned About the Death Penalty, a project of Equal Justice USA.

On the evening of March 11, 2014, Glenn Ford was released from Louisiana's death row after 30 years of captivity for a murder that he did not commit. The prosecution had withheld testimony that would have exonerated Ford and relied on faulty forensic analyses. Unfortunately, Ford's story is not unique. It is one of many cases that exemplify the problems with today's death penalty system.

The Costs of the Death Penalty

Many states are grappling with the systemic dysfunction plaguing the current capital punishment regime, but they are finding it is difficult, if not impossible, to maintain such a program while reconciling its moral, pragmatic, and philosophical failures. The state ought not kill innocent citizens, but the death penalty carries an inherent and undeniable risk of doing precisely that. Whether through mistakes or abuse of power, innocent people routinely get sent to death row.

Some, like Ford, eventually get out: To date, 10 individuals in Louisiana and 144 nationally have been released from death row because they were wrongly convicted. Many others have been executed despite substantial doubts about the verdict.

The fiscal cost of the death penalty pales in comparison to the human cost, but local, state, and federal governments must justify all spending as they struggle with ongoing budgetary shortfalls. John DeRosier, Louisiana District Attorney for Calcasieu Parish, estimated that a capital case in Louisiana is at least three times more costly than a non-death case. Studies in North Carolina, Maryland, California, and many others show that capital punishment is many times more expensive than life without parole, and there's a long history of the death penalty pushing municipal budgets to the brink of bankruptcy and even leading to tax increases.

Submitting the power to kill U.S. citizens to the State is unwise considering [the] history of error and malfeasance.

The fiscal impact of the death penalty is not lost on state governments. But they seem, broadly, more concerned with the fiscal impact than with the death part. Louisiana is currently considering House Bill 71, which is similar to Florida's "Timely Justice Act," which limits the appeals process. Had this legislation passed earlier, it would have likely led to numerous wrongful executions because it shortens the number of appeals available to death row inmates. Cutting the appeals process may, in the end, lead to modest cost savings, but the most expensive step in the death penalty process—pretrial activities and the actual trials—are unaffected by this legislation. And these are precisely the stages that produce wrongful convictions. Evidence proving them wrongful often emerges more than a decade after the initial trial, so the nominal savings are not worth the moral cost of executing an innocent person.

The Government's Ability to Take Life

The expense passed on to the taxpayers and risk of killing innocent people are often both justified by claims that the death penalty saves lives—it supposedly deters murder and provides the justice that murder victims' families deserve. Multiple scientific studies have actually shown that the death penalty doesn't deter murder. Many murder victims' family members are vocally rejecting this program because it retraumatizes them through a decades-long process of trials, appeals, and constant media attention.

There's no greater authority than the power to take life, and our government currently reserves the authority to kill the citizens it's supposed to serve. This is the same fallible government responsible for the Tuskegee Experiment, over-reach including NSA [National Security Agency] spying, and failures such as the Bay of Pigs. Of course, the death toll from wars government either started or intensified is staggering. Submitting the power to kill U.S. citizens to the State is unwise considering this history of error and malfeasance.

And states aren't even complying with the standards that allegedly keep the death penalty from falling afoul of the "cruel and unusual" punishment standard.

The Need for Perfection

Many states can no longer obtain the previously used and approved death penalty drugs. So they've started experimenting on inmates with new drug combinations acquired from secret sources. This has led to botched, torturous executions. In Ohio, Dennis McGwire audibly struggled for 25 minutes before he died, and Clayton Lockett's execution in Oklahoma was postponed after he failed to die after 10 minutes. Indeed, Lockett only met his demise due to a heart attack, 30 minutes after the botched execution. Cruel and unusual?

Glenn Ford could have easily been subjected to the same experiences. Louisiana, like many other states, keeps the source of its death penalty drugs a secret. This secrecy calls into question the legality and validity of the drugs' manufacturers. We are far from the level of government transparency required to limit government abuse, misuse, and power.

Most people will agree that the death penalty system is not perfect—but a program designed to kill guilty U.S. citizens *must* be perfect because the Constitution demands zero errors. To date, 18 states and the District of Columbia have abandoned capital punishment, aware that the system is broken and finally convinced, after years of legislative, judicial, and policy "fixes," that it cannot be mended. Other states still believe they can make capital punishment work properly, but they continue to break an already failed program one "fix" at a time.

Why Death-Penalty Opponents Can't Win

Jonah Goldberg

Jonah Goldberg is editor-at-large of National Review Online *and author of* The Tyranny of Clichés: How Liberals Cheat in the War of Ideas.

On Wednesday, two men were lawfully executed. Both insisted they were innocent. If you've been watching the news or following Kim Kardashian's tweets, you've likely heard of one of these men, Troy Davis.

The other death-penalty "victim," Lawrence Russell Brewer, was until this week the more significant convicted murderer. Brewer was one of the racist goons who infamously tied James Byrd to the back of their truck and dragged him to death in Texas.

The case became a touchstone in the 2000 presidential race because then-Texas governor George W. Bush had refused to sign a "hate crimes" law. The NAACP ran a reprehensible ad during the presidential election trying to insinuate that Bush somehow shared responsibility for the act.

Regardless, Brewer claimed that he was "innocent" because one of his buddies had cut Byrd's throat before they dragged his body around. Forensic evidence directly contradicted this.

Brewer's own statements didn't help either. Such as, "As far as any regrets, no, I have no regrets. . . . I'd do it all over again, to tell you the truth."

Brewer, festooned with tattoos depicting KKK symbols and burning crosses, was "not a sympathetic person" in the words of Gloria Rubac of the Texas Death Penalty Abolition Movement.

Which is why we didn't hear much about him this week. Instead, we heard a great deal about Davis. Many people insist Davis was innocent or that there was "too much doubt" about his guilt to proceed with the execution. Many judges and public officials disagreed, including all nine members of the Supreme Court, who briefly stayed the execution Wednesday night, only to let it proceed hours later.

> *There is no transitive property that renders one heinous murderer less deserving of punishment simply because some other person was exonerated of murder.*

There are many sincere and decent people—on both sides of the ideological spectrum—who are opposed to the death penalty. I consider it an honorable position, even though I disagree with it. I am 100 percent in favor of lawfully executing people who deserve the death penalty and 100 percent opposed to killing people who do not deserve it.

When I say that, many death-penalty opponents angrily respond that I'm missing the point. You can never be certain! Troy Davis proves that!

But he proves no such thing. At best, his case proves that you can't be certain about Davis. You most certainly can be certain about other murderers. If the horrible happens and we learn that Davis really was not guilty, that will be a heart-wrenching revelation. It will cast a negative light on the death penalty, on the Georgia criminal-justice system, and on America.

But you know what it won't do? It won't render Lawrence Russell Brewer one iota less guilty or less deserving of the death penalty. Opponents of capital punishment are extremely selective about the cases they make into public crusades. Strategically, that's smart; you don't want to lead your argument with "unsympathetic persons." But logically, it's problematic. There is no transitive property that renders one heinous murderer less deserving of punishment simply because some other person was exonerated of murder.

Timothy McVeigh killed 168 people including 19 children. He admitted it. How does doubt in Troy Davis's case make McVeigh less deserving of death?

We hear so much about the innocent people who've gotten off death row—thank God—because of new DNA techniques. We hear very little about the criminals who've had their guilt confirmed by the same techniques (or who've declined DNA testing because they know it will remove all doubt). Death-penalty opponents are less eager to debate such cases because they want to delegitimize "the system."

And to be fair, I think this logic cuts against one of the death penalty's greatest rationalizations as well: deterrence. I do believe there's a deterrence effect from the death penalty. But I don't think that's anything more than an ancillary benefit of capital punishment. It's unjust to kill a person simply to send a message to other people who've yet to commit a crime. It is just to execute a person who deserves to be executed.

Opponents of the death penalty believe that no one deserves to be executed. Again, it's an honorable position, but a difficult one to defend politically in a country where the death penalty is popular. So they spend all of their energy cherry-picking cases, gumming up the legal system, and talking about "uncertainty."

That's fine. But until they can explain why we shouldn't have a death penalty when uncertainty isn't an issue—i.e., why McVeigh and Brewer should live—they'll never win the real argument.

Getting Rid of the Death Penalty Would Eliminate Plea Bargains

Debra J. Saunders

Debra J. Saunders is a syndicated columnist for the San Francisco Chronicle.

Recently, editorial page editor John Diaz asked Mark Klaas whether he expects to feel closure if California executes Richard Allen Davis, the man who kidnapped, toyed with and then killed Klaas' 12-year-old daughter, Polly, in 1993. A jury found Davis guilty and sentenced him to death in 1996.

From the early days after Davis snatched Polly from a Petaluma slumber party, Klaas has been a highly visible advocate for strong laws to protect the public, especially children, from career criminals and predators like Davis. He had come to the *San Francisco Chronicle* with other opponents of Proposition 34, the ballot measure that would end California's death penalty and resentence California's 700-plus death row inmates to life without parole.

Klaas' answer may surprise you. He sadly shook his head and answered. "Is it going to bring any closure to me? No."

But, Klaas added, Davis "will no longer be able to run his website." Young girls no longer will write to him.

The Movement to End the Death Penalty

It turns out the Canadian Coalition Against the Death Penalty hosts a Richard Allen Davis home page, on which the convicted killer displays "hand-painted wood hobby craft items," which he made, and posts photos of himself. Davis also wonders whether there's anyone out there who wants to know who he really is, and he asks, "For someone like myself, can one ever fall back in love with life again?"

Davis invites interested parties to write to him at San Quentin.

Klaas wants to see Davis executed, he told me later, because the man who killed his daughter should have no influence in this world. That, he emphasized, is "what's supposed to stop."

Good luck with that. Thanks to a highly successful defense lobby and federal judges who have stalled the enforcement of California law, only 13 of the state's death row inmates have been executed since 1992.

So now the folks behind Proposition 34 argue that California's death penalty is "too costly" and "broken beyond repair." End the death penalty, they say, and Californians will save money on sentencing trials, costly appeals and "special death row housing."

The anti-death penalty lobby is asking Californians to disarm themselves unilaterally.

The nonpartisan Legislative Analyst's Office estimates that the savings could amount to $100 million annually in the first few years.

There's a caveat with that number.

The Importance of Plea Bargains

The Legislative Analyst's Office also noted that it cannot compute the financial effect that might follow if murderers stopped pleading guilty and making plea bargains that enable them to avoid death row.

As Klaas sees it, the anti-death penalty lobby is asking Californians to disarm themselves unilaterally.

He cited cases like that of John Gardner. After the convicted sex offender was arrested for the murder of 17-year-old Chelsea King in 2010, Gardner went for a deal. He admitted to killing King and also to the 2009 murder and attempted rape of 14-year-old Amber Dubois. Gardner even led authorities to Amber's bones.

Parents Brent and Kelly King agreed to the plea bargain because, they said in a statement covered by CBS News, their family had been through "unthinkable hell" for 14 months. "We couldn't imagine the confession to Amber's murder never seeing the light of day, leaving an eternal question mark," they said.

"You take the death penalty off the table," Klaas told the *Chronicle*, and communities will be held hostage to the fear and uncertainty that follow when a young person goes missing. "Crimes will not be solved. Victims will not be recovered."

Without the death penalty, it is doubtful that Jared Lee Loughner would have pleaded guilty to a 2011 shooting in Tucson, Ariz., during which he killed six and wounded then-Rep. Gabrielle Giffords. Given his history of mental illness, it's not clear whether Loughner would have been found guilty.

The Need for the Death Penalty

Even when it doesn't work, the death penalty works.

California prosecutors and California juries do not reach the death penalty lightly. Sacramento Deputy District Attorney Anne Marie Schubert estimates that death row inmates represent less than 2 percent of those convicted for murder.

At least with the death penalty on the books, there's a good chance that some of the worst offenders will agree to a sentence of life without parole in order to avoid lethal injection.

In such cases, there is quick resolution and certainty of outcome, and victims' families need not worry about an offender's getting off, because the defendant has no grounds for appeals. All of the outcomes that the anti-death penalty lobby extols—cheaper, faster and more certain—exist only because of the death penalty.

Why would Californians want to get rid of it?

Organizations to Contact

The editors have compiled the following list of organizations concerned with the issues debated in this book. The descriptions are derived from materials provided by the organizations. All have publications or information available for interested readers. The list was compiled on the date of publication of the present volume; names, addresses, phone and fax numbers, and e-mail and Internet addresses may change. Be aware that many organizations take several weeks or longer to respond to inquiries, so allow as much time as possible.

American Civil Liberties Union (ACLU)
125 Broad St., 18th Floor, New York, NY   10004
(212) 549-2500 • fax: (212) 549-2646
e-mail: aclu@aclu.org
website: www.aclu.org

The American Civil Liberties Union (ACLU) believes that capital punishment violates the US Constitution's ban on cruel and unusual punishment as well as the requirements of due process and equal protection under the law. The ACLU Capital Punishment Project (CPP) works to abolish the death penalty nationally through direct representation as well as through strategic litigation, advocacy, public education, and mentoring and training programs for capital defense teams. The ACLU publishes numerous papers on the topic, including "The Case Against the Death Penalty."

Amnesty International USA
5 Penn Plaza, New York, NY   10001
(212) 807-8400 • fax: (212) 627-1451
e-mail: aimember@aiusa.org
website: www.amnestyusa.org

Amnesty International USA's Abolish the Death Penalty campaign seeks the abolishment of the death penalty worldwide. Its most recent activities have been aimed at decreasing the use of the death penalty internationally, including in the United States, and increasing the number of countries that have removed the death penalty as an option for punishment. It also serves as an advocate in individual clemency cases. Amnesty International USA publishes news, fact sheets, and reports, including "Death Sentences and Executions 2013," which are available on its website.

Campaign to End the Death Penalty (CEDP)
PO Box 25730, Chicago, IL   60625
(773) 955-4841
website: www.nodeathpenalty.org

The Campaign to End the Death Penalty (CEDP) is a national grassroots organization dedicated to the abolition of capital punishment in the United States. CEDP is involved in death row cases, does research and outreach, and protests executions. CEDP publishes updates on death row cases, fact sheets about capital punishment in the United States, and a newsletter, *The New Abolitionist.*

Crime Prevention Research Center (CPRC)
212 Lafayette Ave., Swarthmore, PA   19081
e-mail: info@crimeresearch.org
website: www.crimepreventionresearchcenter.org

The Crime Prevention Research Center (CPRC) is a research and education organization dedicated to conducting academic quality research on the relationship between laws regulating the ownership or use of guns, crime, and public safety. CPRC aims to educate the public and policy makers and takes a stand in favor of the death penalty. CPRC publishes numerous articles available at its website, including "What Does the Research on the Death Penalty Actually Show?"

Criminal Justice Legal Foundation (CJLF)
2131 L St., Sacramento, CA   95816
(916) 446-0345
website: www.cjlf.org

The Criminal Justice Legal Foundation (CJLF) was established in 1982 as a nonprofit, public interest law organization dedicated to restoring a balance between the rights of crime victims and the criminally accused. CJLF works to encourage precedent-setting decisions that recognize the constitutional rights of victims and law-abiding society and enable the deterrent effect of swift and decisive criminal justice. CJLF sponsors the blog *Crime & Consequences*, and its website offers links to various transcripts, articles, and working papers, including "The Death Penalty and Plea Bargaining to Life Sentences."

Death Penalty Information Center (DPIC)
1015 18th St. NW, Suite 704, Washington, DC 20036
(202) 289-2275 • fax: (202) 289-7336
e-mail: dpic@deathpenaltyinfo.org
website: www.deathpenaltyinfo.org

The Death Penalty Information Center (DPIC) is a nonprofit organization that provides the media and public with information concerning capital punishment. DPIC opposes the death penalty because it believes that capital punishment is discriminatory, costly to taxpayers, and may result in innocent persons being put to death. DPIC publishes reports and facts about the death penalty, as well as annual reports.

Justice for All (JFA)
PO Box 55159, Houston, TX 77255
(713) 935-9300
e-mail: info@jfa.net
website: www.jfa.net

Justice for All (JFA) is an all-volunteer, nonprofit criminal justice reform organization that supports the death penalty. JFA acts as an advocate for change in a criminal justice system that it believes is inadequate in protecting the lives and property of law-abiding citizens. It also provides links to stories about victims and information about the victims of death row inmates.

National Coalition to Abolish the Death Penalty

1620 L St. NW, Suite 250, Washington, DC   20036
(202) 331-4090
website: www.ncadp.org

The National Coalition to Abolish the Death Penalty's mission is to abolish the death penalty in the United States and support efforts to abolish the death penalty worldwide. The National Coalition to Abolish the Death Penalty works to repeal the death penalty state by state through strategic planning, campaign development, and training services. To further its goal, the Coalition publishes blogs, information packets, pamphlets, research materials, and the quarterly newsletter *Life-Lines*.

US Department of Justice (DOJ)

950 Pennsylvania Ave. NW, Washington, DC   20530-0001
(202) 514-2000
e-mail: AskDOJ@usdoj.gov
website: www.usdoj.gov

The mission of the US Department of Justice (DOJ) is to enforce the law and defend the interests of the United States according to the law. DOJ works to ensure public safety against foreign and domestic threats, to provide federal leadership in preventing and controlling crime, to seek just punishment for those guilty of unlawful behavior, and to ensure fair and impartial administration of justice for all Americans. Publications available on its website include annual capital punishment statistical tables as well as articles about current DOJ activities and links to DOJ agencies, such as the Civil Rights Division.

Bibliography

Books

John D. Bessler   *Cruel & Unusual: The American Death Penalty and the Founders' Eighth Amendment.* Boston: Northeastern University Press, 2012.

Robert M. Bohm   *Capital Punishment's Collateral Damage.* Durham, NC: Carolina Academic Press, 2013.

Raymond Bonner   *Anatomy of Injustice: A Murder Case Gone Wrong.* New York: Alfred A. Knopf, 2012.

Kathleen A. Cairns   *Proof of Guilt: Barbara Graham and the Politics of Executing Women in America.* Lincoln: University of Nebraska Press, 2013.

Martin Clancy and Tim O'Brien   *Murder at the Supreme Court: Lethal Crimes and Landmark Cases.* Amherst, NY: Prometheus Books, 2013.

David R. Dow   *The Autobiography of an Execution.* New York: Twelve, 2010.

David Garland   *Peculiar Institution: America's Death Penalty in an Age of Abolition.* Cambridge, MA: Belknap Press of Harvard University Press, 2010.

Brandon L. Garrett — *Convicting the Innocent: Where Criminal Prosecutions Go Wrong.* Cambridge, MA: Harvard University Press, 2011.

Bruce Jackson and Diane Christian — *In This Timeless Time: Living and Dying on Death Row in America.* Chapel Hill: University of North Carolina Press, 2012.

Richard S. Jaffe — *Quest for Justice: Defending the Damned.* Far Hills, NJ: New Horizon Press, 2012.

Charles Lane — *Stay of Execution: Saving the Death Penalty from Itself.* Lanham, MD: Rowman & Littlefield, 2010.

Eric Lose — *Living on Death Row.* El Paso, TX: LFB Scholarly Publishing, 2014.

Andrea D. Lyon — *Angel of Death Row: My Life as a Death Penalty Defense Lawyer.* New York: Kaplan Publishing, 2010.

Jen Marlowe and Martina Davis-Correia — *I Am Troy Davis.* Chicago: Haymarket Books, 2013.

David M. Oshinsky — *Capital Punishment on Trial: Furman v. Georgia and the Death Penalty in Modern America.* Lawrence: University Press of Kansas, 2010.

Louis J. Palmer Jr. — *The Death Penalty in the United States: A Complete Guide to Federal and State Laws.* Jefferson, NC: McFarland & Company, 2014.

Michael L. Perlin   *Mental Disability and the Death Penalty: The Shame of the States.* Lanham, MD: Rowman & Littlefield, 2013.

Wilbert Rideau   *In the Place of Justice: A Story of Punishment and Deliverance.* New York: Alfred A. Knopf, 2010.

James D. Slack   *Abortion, Execution, and the Consequences of Taking Life.* New Brunswick, NJ: Transaction Publishers, 2014.

Periodicals and Internet Sources

Allen Ault   "Ordering Death in Georgia Prisons," *Newsweek*, September 25, 2011. www.newsweek.com.

Marc Bookman   "The Confessions of Innocent Men," *Atlantic*, August 6, 2013.

Boston Globe   "New Hampshire Should Abolish Death Penalty," April 16, 2014.

Andrew Cohen   "The Problems with the Death Penalty Are Already Crystal Clear," *Atlantic*, May 5, 2014.

Boer Deng and Dahlia Lithwick   "Liberal Guilt," *Slate*, May 9, 2014. www.slate.com.

Richard C. Dieter   "Struck By Lightning: The Continuing Arbitrariness of the Death Penalty Thirty-Five Years After Its Re-instatement in 1976," Death Penalty Information Center, July 2011. www.deathpenaltyinfo.org.

Matt Ford — "Can Europe End the Death Penalty in America?," *Atlantic*, February 18, 2014.

Alex Gibney, Robert Redford, and Susan Sarandon — "Redford, Gibney, Sarandon: Why Conservatives Should Oppose the Flawed Death Penalty, Too," *Salon*, March 21, 2014. www.salon.com.

Stephen John Hartnett — "5 Things You Should Know About the History of the Death Penalty," *AlterNet*, April 15, 2013. www.alternet.org.

Richard Kim — "The Oklahoma Way of Death," *Nation*, May 26, 2014.

Pema Levy — "An Unlikely Conservative Cause: Abolish the Death Penalty," *Newsweek*, May 14, 2014. www.newsweek.com.

Tanya Lewis — "Why Lethal Injection Drugs Don't Always Work as Expected," *Huffington Post*, May 1, 2014. www.huffingtonpost.com.

Dahlia Lithwick — "When the Death Penalty Turns into Torture," *Slate*, April 30, 2014. www.slate.com.

John R. Lott Jr. — "Another Round in the Death-Penalty Debate," *National Review Online*, May 13, 2014. www.nationalreview.com.

Matt McCarthy — "What's the Best Way to Execute Someone?," *Slate*, March 27, 2014. www.slate.com.

Laura Moye — "Supreme Court Must Not Allow Executions of the Mentally Impaired," CNN, August 8, 2012. www.cnn.com.

New York Times — "State-Sponsored Horror in Oklahoma," April 30, 2014.

Leon Neyfakh — "The Conservative Case Against the Death Penalty," *Boston Globe*, May 25, 2014.

Marvin Olasky — "Better Off Dead?: Capital Punishment Versus (a Horrifying) Life Without Parole," *Townhall*, October 15, 2013. www.townhall.com.

Debra J. Saunders — "If Lethal Injection Is Torture, Who's Responsible?," *Townhall*, May 2, 2014. www.townhall.com.

Liliana Segura — "Florida's Gruesome Execution Theater," *Washington Post*, March 19, 2014.

Peter Singer — "The Death Penalty—Again," *Project Syndicate*, October 12, 2011. www.project-syndicate.org.

Jacob Sullum — "A Lethal Injection of Reality," *Reason*, May 7, 2014. www.reason.com.

Mark Tooley — "Jesus and the Death Penalty," *American Spectator*, May 3, 2014.

David Von Drehle   "More Innocent People on Death Row than Estimated," *Time*, April 28, 2014.

Paul Waldman   "Where the Death Penalty Stands," *American Prospect*, April 18, 2014.

Lane Wallace   "Are All Murderers Mentally Ill?," *Atlantic*, December 3, 2010.

Index

CPSIA information can be obtained
at www.ICGtesting.com
Printed in the USA
FFOW05n1701300315